Jane Eyre

Charlotte Brontë

Notes by Karen Sayer

 Longman   York Press

The right of Karen Sayer to be identified as Author of this Work has been asserted by her in accordance with the Copyright, Designs and Patents Act 1988

YORK PRESS
322 Old Brompton Road, London SW5 9JH

PEARSON EDUCATION LIMITED
Edinburgh Gate, Harlow,
Essex CM20 2JE, United Kingdom
Associated companies, branches and representatives throughout the world

First published 1998
Third impression 2001

ISBN 0-582-32920-5

Designed by Vicki Pacey, Trojan Horse, London
Phototypeset by Gem Graphics, Trenance, Mawgan Porth, Cornwall
Colour reproduction and film output by Spectrum Colour
Produced by Pearson Education North Asia Limited, Hong Kong

CONTENTS

PART ONE

INTRODUCTION How to Study a Novel   5
              Reading *Jane Eyre: An Autobiography*   6

PART TWO

SUMMARIES   Note on the Text   7
              Synopsis   7
              Detailed Summaries   9

PART THREE

CRITICAL APPROACHES
              Characterisation   41
                Jane Eyre   42
                Mr Rochester and St John Rivers   42
                Minor Characters   44
              Themes   47
                Moral Courage   47
                Search for Identity   48
                Self-fulfilment   48
                Social Class   49
                The Marriage Market   50
                Quest for Love   50
                Religious Faith   51
              Narrative Techniques   51
                Structure   51
                Narrative and Point of View   52
              Language and Style   54
              Imagery and Symbolism   55

PART FOUR

TEXTUAL ANALYSIS
              Text 1: The Red-Room   58
              Text 2: Rochester's Proposal   61
              Text 3: St John's Proposal   64

PART FIVE

B ACKGROUND   Charlotte Brontë and her Works   68
Historical Background   69
Literary Background   70

PART SIX

C RITICAL HISTORY
Reception and Early Critical Reviews   72
Early Twentieth-Century Views   72
Marxist Criticism   73
Feminist Criticism   73
Contemporary Approaches   74

PART SEVEN

B ROADER PERSPECTIVES
Further Reading   76
Chronology   77
Literary Terms   80
Author of this Note   81

PART ONE

INTRODUCTION

HOW TO STUDY A NOVEL

Studying a novel on your own requires self-discipline and a carefully thought-out work plan in order to be effective.

- You will need to read the novel more than once. Start reading it quickly for pleasure, then read it slowly and thoroughly.

- On your second reading make detailed notes on the plot, characters and themes of the novel. Further readings will generate new ideas and help you to memorise the details of the story.

- Some of the characters will develop as the plot unfolds. How do your responses towards them change during the course of the novel?

- Think about how the novel is narrated. From whose point of view are events described?

- A novel may or may not present events chronologically: the time scheme may be a key to its structure and organisation.

- What part do the settings play in the novel?

- Are words, images or incidents repeated so as to give the work a pattern? Do such patterns help you to understand the novel's themes?

- Identify what styles of language are used in the novel.

- What is the effect of the novel's ending? Is the action completed and closed, or left incomplete and open?

- Does the novel present a moral and just world?

- Cite exact sources for all quotations, whether from the text itself or from critical commentaries. Wherever possible find your own examples from the novel to back up your opinions.

- Always express your ideas in your own words.

This York Note offers an introduction to *Jane Eyre* and cannot substitute for close reading of the text and the study of secondary sources.

It is easy to identify with *Jane Eyre*, for though the novel was written over a century and a half ago Jane expresses a young girl's longing for fulfilment, and fulfilment on her own terms – a concept very much at odds with the dictates of society in her own day. Jane's fierce rebellion is a constant throughout the book, and though she appears to follow customary practice, she actually grows to maturity as a passionate and strong-willed woman whose aspirations confound convention.

Jane Eyre is full of dramatic contrasts, in which the ordinary and everyday are set against the gothic, and is so packed with supernatural detail, coincidence and magic that it seems to be a fairytale even though it is built upon the foundations of everyday life. The narrative is forceful, vivid, and leaves a lasting impression of both anguish and delight. It is, however, carefully structured, controlled and coherent. It shows us how Brontë sought to write not only about what she observed, but also what was hidden and unseen. The form has been dictated by the theme and that theme is deeply felt.

As soon as *Jane Eyre* was published it became immensely popular, though it attracted vehement criticism. This was because of its attack on Evangelicalism and, given its quite explicit portrayal of physical and emotional desires, because of its coarse morality. With hindsight, the Victorian assessment seems harsh, for though Jane is in part an advocate for her sex, she also has to combine passion with duty before she can live happily ever after.

The novel does not have a moral as such, Charlotte Brontë always resisted writing for a purpose. Rather it consists of a deep psychological insight into an individual's emotional and intellectual needs.

PART TWO

SUMMARIES

Begun in 1846, *Jane Eyre* was initially published in October 1847 by Smith, Elder & Co. in three volumes under the supposed editorship of 'Currer Bell'. The novel was so popular that a second edition appeared in January 1848, followed by a third in April of the same year. Brontë's publishers wanted her to illustrate the third edition, but she refused because she felt that she lacked the necessary skill. Also, she did not believe that her characters ought to have portraits because they were, 'mostly unattractive in looks'. The final version to be published during Charlotte Brontë's lifetime was a one-volume edition in 1850.

In each edition, except the last, corrections and small revisions were made by the author; however, each new edition also saw the introduction of new errors and misprints. Twentieth-century editors have often taken the liberty of correcting the text, especially in matters of spelling, punct-uation and apparently accidental departures from earlier editions. The third edition sanctioned by Brontë therefore now forms the basis of most modern imprints of the novel, but many editors also refer to the manuscript used by the printers to set the first edition.

Unfortunately, the earlier Penguin Classics edition of 1966 is now out of print, but is worth trying to get hold of as Q.D. Leavis's introduction and notes still provide the reader with some of the most thoughtful and thorough commentary available. One of the most useful modern editions is the Penguin Classics edition of 1996 edited, with introduction and notes by Michael Mason; the text of this edition has been used in compiling this Note.

SYNOPSIS

At the beginning of the novel Jane Eyre is an orphan who lives with her well-to-do aunt, Mrs Reed, and cousins, Eliza, John and Georgiana. Jane is constantly bullied by her cousins, and her aunt always assumes that she is the guilty party whenever there is a fight. On one occasion Mrs Reed locks Jane in a room that is reputedly haunted, as punishment for a crime that she did not commit. Jane's nerves are shattered and the servants' apothecary is called in. Immeasurably unhappy, Jane is deeply relieved to discover that he has recommended she be sent away to boarding school. Before she leaves she makes friends with Bessie, the nursemaid, and wins a psychological battle against her aunt.

Jane is sent to Lowood, a school for clergymen's daughters, where she makes friends with another pupil, Helen Burns, and the mistress, Miss Temple. Helen, who is deeply religious, gentle and forbearing, teaches Jane the value of self-control. However, the conditions at the school are appalling and, when the girls become sick, Helen dies of consumption. The school is reformed and Jane stays on for a total of eight years, as pupil, then as assistant teacher. When Miss Temple leaves to marry, Jane begins to find life at the school restrictive and advertises for a new job.

She is soon offered a place by a Mrs Fairfax as governess to 'a little girl, under ten years of age' at double her Lowood salary, and sets out to take up her new position as quickly as she can. When she arrives at Thornfield Hall she finds that Mrs Fairfax is housekeeper to the master, Edward Fairfax Rochester, and that the little girl, Adèle Varens, is his ward. The place suits Jane and she settles in quickly, but for some time does not see Rochester, until out on an errand one day she meets him as he rides towards Thornfield. His horse slips on some ice and he is obliged to seek her aid.

As they become better acquainted Jane begins to feel drawn to Rochester; he is equally attracted by her intelligence and wit. While she is away from the hall visiting her dying aunt she misses him and he tries to make her jealous by pretending that he is going to marry a local heiress, Miss Blanche Ingram. In the end, despite the differences in their station and age, Rochester finally proposes and Jane accepts. The match is ill-omened, however, and their wedding is interrupted by the arrival of Mr Richard Mason who declares that Rochester is already married to his sister, Bertha Mason. It becomes clear that there is indeed a Mrs Rochester, but that she is a mad-woman, kept under lock and key in the attic of Thornfield. Rochester pleads for Jane to go abroad with him as his mistress, but she cannot bring herself to stay and slips away from the hall before anyone can stop her.

Jane wanders destitute for some days. No-one will help her or give her work until she is finally taken in by a clergyman, St John Rivers, and his sisters, Diana and Mary, who find Jane half-starved at their door. As she recovers from her ordeal she makes friends with the sisters and St John offers her a job as the village schoolmistress. She works at the school under the assumed name of Jane Elliott, but St John discovers her real name on one of her drawings. Through this he is able to tell her that she is related to him and his sisters and that she has inherited a fortune from her uncle. She insists on sharing the money equally with her new-found family and hopes to be treated as their sister.

St John is a cold ambitious man who hopes to become a missionary and, in the end, he asks Jane to marry him and travel to India as his help-mate. Jane says that though she might help him in his missionary work she cannot marry him because he does not love her. As he presses her on the matter and she begins to give way, she hears Rochester calling to her. Jane decides that she must find out what has become of Rochester before she can do anything else and travels back to Thornfield.

When she reaches Thornfield she discovers that the house has been razed to the ground and further investigation reveals that the hall has been burnt down by Mrs Rochester. Edward Rochester is alive, but, in the process of trying to save his wife, has suffered terrible injuries. Jane determines to find him and, though he is maimed and blind, they finally marry. The novel closes with an account of their married life and a brief summary of what has happened to Diana, Mary and St John Rivers.

VOLUME I

CHAPTER 1   **Jane flies at Master John**

Jane Eyre has not been allowed to sit with her Aunt Reed and cousins after dinner and is therefore reading Bewick's *History of British Birds* on her own when she is interrupted by her cousin, John. He picks on her and when he throws a book at her she hits her head on the door. Bleeding, she begins calling him names, and they get into a fight. His sisters, Eliza and Georgiana, run for Mrs Reed who comes in with the nursemaid, Bessie, and her servant, Abbot. Jane is taken away to 'the red-room'.

This chapter is one of the earliest accounts given by a child from a child's **point of view** in English fiction. Though it is actually being narrated in retrospect by the mature Jane Rochester several years after the close of Vol. III, Chapter 11, it nonetheless provides us with a highly suggestive portrait of Jane Eyre's childish thoughts and feelings.

The references to Bewick help disclose Jane's state of mind. The book is full of images of shipwrecks, storms, Arctic wastes, high mountain reaches, death and disaster. Her inferior position within the Reed family is made brutally clear through her fight with John. John's introduction **foreshadows** his rather unfortunate end in Vol. II, Chapter 6.

Bewick's *History of British Birds* (1804) includes the quotations used (introduction of Vol. II, p. xii) and many detailed vignettes

Where ... Hebrides from James Thomson, *The Seasons* (1726–30)

Pamela novel by Samuel Richardson (1740)

Henry Earl of Moreland John Wesley's abridgement of Henry Brooke, *The Fool of Quality* (1781)

Goldsmith's *History of Rome* Oliver Goldsmith's abridgement of *The Roman History* (1772)

CHAPTER 2   Jane is locked in the red-room

Miss Abbot and Bessie lock Jane in the red-room. Jane is initially angry, but soon becomes frightened as dusk falls. She thinks that the room is haunted and that her uncle, Mr Reed, who died in the room is about to come for her. She screams out in terror and Miss Abbot and Bessie come to see what is wrong, but Jane's aunt leaves her in the room for another hour. Jane passes out.

In this chapter the supernatural mixes with mundane detail about the Reeds, Jane's origin and background. She is just ten and her fear of the 'red-room', connected as it is with death, seems quite natural. In addition to the child's point of view, however, we are also given a privileged insight into her position by the adult Jane who looks back and reflects on the scene.

The fact that Jane is described as 'a mad cat' and is made to sit fixedly on a chair as part of her punishment allows us to draw parallels between Jane and Mrs Rochester. We also learn that Jane can be quite superstitious as well as passionate, and she battles with both tendencies throughout the course of the novel.

cover deceitfulness
Marseilles stiff cotton fabric
race blood-relations

CHAPTER 3   Jane says that she would like to go to school

Jane wakes up to find that the servants' apothecary, Mr Lloyd, has been called to look at her. Bessie tries to cheer her up, but Jane cannot be tempted by either tarts or books. Mr Lloyd asks her why she is so sad and she tries to explain. He asks her if she would like to leave and though she would not like to go to her father's family – whom she assumes are poor – she says she would like to go to school.

We find out more about Jane's mother and Bessie's ballad reflects Jane's own condition as a 'poor orphan child'. Bessie's story about the 'great, black dog' is picked up in Chapter 12, and the idea that all the fairies have left England is reiterated in Chapter 13. We can therefore begin to guess that Bessie is very important to Jane. The nursemaid does in fact seem to care for Miss Eyre after all, and this sets the tone for their reconciliation in Chapter 4.

Because we only ever receive information from Jane's **point of view** and because we get to know her deepest thoughts and feelings we tend to assume that she is a reliable narrator, but she is not always a sympathetic character. She is a precocious girl and there are moments when the reader feels quite sorry for Mrs Reed. Jane's initial response to the plight of the poor and her adult reflection on this serve to remind us that she is still just a child, brought up by the indolent and snobbish Reeds.

apothecary medical practitioner who could dispense medicines, but not a qualified doctor
I ought to forgive ... did reference to Luke 23:34

Gulliver's Travels satire by Jonathan Swift (1726)
In the days ... ago popular song, Edward Ransford (c.1840)
My feet ... child unknown ballad
backboards devices meant to improve the way you sit or stand
toad general insult

CHAPTER 4   Jane meets Mr Brocklehurst, wins a psychological battle against her aunt and makes up with Bessie

It is decided that Jane shall go to school. Jane continues to stand up for herself and starts to talk back to her aunt, who tells her cousins to stay away from her. Though the arrangements for sending Jane away seem to take a long time, she finally meets her future headmaster, Mr Brocklehurst. Deeply upset when her aunt blackens her reputation, Jane tells Mrs Reed what she thinks of her. Mrs Reed is frightened and Jane exults in her first real victory over her aunt. Jane, still overexcited, goes out into the garden and when Bessie comes to fetch her, Jane makes up with the nurse who likes the girl's new-found self-confidence.

We are never surprised by Jane's behaviour as we move through the novel because the foundation is laid for every action and response. Jane's dislike of the company who turn up for Christmas prefigures her uneasiness at the arrival of guests at Thornfield in Vol. II, Chapter 2. Though Jane swears never to call Mrs Reed 'aunt' again, when she does so, in Vol. II, Chapter 6, she is quite self-conscious about it. We see all the characters in the novel from Jane's **point of view** and a perfect example of this can be found in the way our opinion of Bessie changes as Jane begins to see her differently.

Mr Brocklehurst is described by Jane as if he were the big bad wolf from 'Little Red Riding Hood' – c.f. Vol. II, Chapter 4. This reflects the influence of Bessie's stories on Jane and the child's point of view, but the implication is also that Mr Brocklehurst is a liar: when he says he is consistent we should not believe him. Jane's replies to his questions about the Bible, heaven and hell are supposed to imply criticism of his highly conventional theology. However, they also suggest that Jane has not read the Gospels, which would have taught her to forgive those who harm her, as Helen Burns points out in Chapter 6.

waited awaited

stirred my corruption (dialect) made me angry

graven image (biblical) idol

traffic trade

to take ... flesh Ezekiel, 11:19 and 36:26

Child's Guide based on a monthly tract, *The Children's Friend*

racy high quality

onding on snaw from Walter Scott, *The Heart of Midlothian*, 'pelting with snow'

CHAPTER 5   Jane goes to school

Jane leaves Gateshead on 19 January. She arrives at Lowood school in the dark, rain and wind. She is so tired and overexcited that she cannot eat any supper. The next day the girls sit down to breakfast but the porridge is burnt and they cannot eat it. Much to their surprise the superintendent, Miss Temple, therefore decides to serve the girls lunch. During her first day Jane meets another pupil who tells her about the school, its principles and its teachers.

This chapter sets the scene for the Lowood section of the book and the next stage in Jane's life. It is therefore largely **expository**; much of the information is provided by the dialogue that takes place between Jane and the other pupil – Helen Burns. The harsh regime at the school is indicated by the cold weather. Helen Burns's character is suggested by her choice of reading matter.

mess prepared dish

organ of Veneration term from phrenology, the nineteenth-century practice of linking the skull's features to an individual's character

irids plural of iris

front forehead

Rasselass Samuel Johnson, *Rasselas* (1759), didactic romance about the aims of human life

rusty rancid

CHAPTER 6   Jane begins her career at Lowood

Jane is enrolled as a member of the fourth class and begins her lessons. As she sits sewing, she sees her new friend participating in a history lesson. It appears that the girl, Burns, is being picked on by the teacher, Miss Scatcherd, even though the girl is very good at the subject. At one point Burns is flogged, but takes it stoically. In the evening, Jane speaks to Burns and finds out that her first name is Helen. Jane asks her why she puts up with Miss Scatcherd's bullying and she explains the principles of endurance, duty and self-sacrifice to Jane, as based on the New Testament Gospels.

> The chapter largely consists of the conversation that takes place between Jane and Helen. Though this dialogue covers some complex theological ground, it is nonetheless quite naturalistic and provides us with a deep insight into Helen's character. Helen offers one solution to Jane's problem – the need to quell her passionate nature – and Jane does learn from her, as we begin to see in the following chapters. But Helen's faith is also essentially inward-looking, as indicated by her tendency to slip into reverie, and potentially death-willing; she looks forward to death as an elevation, 'I live in calm, looking to the end'.

stops punctuation
mark embroider
'the Bible bids us ... evil' based on Christ's sermon on the mount, Matthew 5–7
'like Felix ... convenient season' Acts 24
'Love your enemies ... use you' Matthew 5:44
'the time ... corruptible bodies' I Corinthians 15:50–3

CHAPTER 7   Mr Brocklehurst tells the other school girls that Jane is a liar

It is winter and all the girls suffer from the cold and hunger, especially when they walk to church. The big girls hog the fire and take most of the little girls' food. Eventually the proprietor, Mr Brocklehurst, visits the school. He criticises Miss Temple for giving the girls lunch, picks on one of the girls, Julia Severn, for having naturally curly hair, even though his own daughters curl theirs artificially, and as soon as he sees Jane makes her sit in front of the whole school while he calls her a liar.

Jane's conflict with Mr Brocklehurst was foreshadowed in Vol. I, Chapter 4. Mr Brocklehurst never lives up to his Evangelical principles and his character is formed in direct opposition to that of the other clergyman in the novel, St John Rivers. Brocklehurst is described (in Chapter 4) as 'a black pillar', whereas St John is 'marble' (Vol. III, Chapter 9); Brocklehurst is a hypocrite, unlike St John who is ruthlessly consistent and as 'inexorable as death' (Vol. III, Chapter 5).

In this instance Brocklehurst's inconsistency is made clear in his attack on Julia Severn and the entrance of his fashionably dressed wife and daughters. Moreover, his religious principles are clearly impossible to live up to as he will not brook a girl to conform either to the world or to nature. Jane is falsely accused as she was in Chapter 1 and begins to panic as she did in Chapter 2, but by this point, thanks to Helen Burns's help and Miss Temple's example, Jane proves that she can control her emotions and take her punishment.

starved frozen

'the fifth, sixth ... Matthew' chapters that contain the sermon on the mount

Eutychus Acts 2:9–10, Eutychus falls asleep during one of St Paul's sermons and apparently falls to his death from a window, but is revived

'Coming Man' man likely to achieve eminence

take up their cross Mark 8:34

man shall not live by bread alone ... God Matthew 4:4

'if ye suffer ... happy are ye' Luke 6:21 and I Peter 3:14

Grace idea that God will redeem certain individuals and not others

cup and platter Matthew 13:25–6

'kingdom is not of this world' John 18:36

false front hairpiece

'kneels before Juggernaut' suggests that Jane prays to the Hindu god Krishna

'even as the Jews ... round her' John 5:2–4

CHAPTER 8   Jane recovers her reputation

After the school is dismissed, Jane is left alone and breaks down in tears. Her friend Helen comes to comfort her and when Miss Temple finds them she takes them to her room. Jane tells her story to Miss Temple who writes to Mr Lloyd, the apothecary, for corroboration. When he writes back, she gets the whole school together and publicly clears Jane's reputation. Jane is promoted to a higher class and goes on to learn French and drawing.

> Helen's conversation with Jane shows that self-reliance can come from faith; self-respect and individuality are stressed here above all else. The fact that Jane takes some of this teaching on board becomes clear in her visit to Gateshead and flight from Thornfield later on in the novel. When she comes to tell her story to Miss Temple we can see that Jane has already learnt to control some of her worst excesses thanks to Helen. Helen exemplifies the Christian ideal of turning one's cheek, forgiving one's enemies and meek endurance. She is a model of morality and of learning, but Jane is doubtful about the validity of Helen's example: 'in the tranquillity she imparted there was an alloy of inexpressible sadness'. Helen's faith makes her turn away from life and Helen's subsequent illness and death is **foreshadowed** several times.

Barmecide supper fantasy feast
Cuyp-like after the seventeenth-century Dutch landscape painter Albert Cuyp
currently fluently
'Better is a dinner ... therewith' Proverbs 15:17

CHAPTER 9   **Helen Burns dies**

As winter gives way to spring, so most of the pupils begin to fall ill. More than half of them need nursing and the rest are left to look after themselves. Jane remains fairly well and can play in the spring sunshine, but many of the girls die and Helen becomes very sick. One evening Jane slips in to visit Helen, determined to see her friend before she dies. They talk a little and Jane is amazed by Helen's faith. Helen asks Jane to stay with her and as they sleep so Helen dies.

> In this chapter we see the first direct reference to the reader: 'True, reader'. This is a device which recurs several times throughout the remainder of the novel, the last being: 'Reader, I married him' Vol. III, Chapter 12. This device creates a close bond between the narrator and the reader and draws the latter into the story. These petitions to the reader always come at moments of heightened intensity or action,

often adding detail to a relationship or Jane's thoughts at that moment. In this case it acts as a supplement to the narrative, and highlights just how important Helen Burns is to Jane.

The conversation is convincing and naturalistic and there is considerable pathos in Helen's death. Helen is doomed to die young and her faith is shaped by this. As suggested in Chapter 6, Helen's religion is death-willing, she expects to be happier dead than alive, and Jane cannot understand this. Death and sickness are contrasted very sharply in this chapter with health and the will to live, both in the girl's environment and in their beliefs. In the morning Jane is merely sleeping while Helen is starkly '– dead'.

'ing' (dialect) waterside field

fog-bred pestilence from the 'miasma' theory of disease, later replaced by idea of bacterial and viral infection

drug aromatic medicine

pastille substance burnt for aromatic smoke

likely (dialect) suitable

'long home' death

Resurgam (Latin) 'I shall rise again'

CHAPTER 10   **The school is reformed. When Miss Temple marries, Jane decides to advertise and is offered a job**

The outbreak of typhus leads to an enquiry into the running of Lowood and the school is reformed. Jane stays there a further eight years, six as a pupil and two as an assistant teacher. After Miss Temple leaves, in order to marry a clergyman, Jane realises that it is time to go out into the world at large. She advertises for a new post and receives a letter from a Mrs Fairfax offering her a situation looking after a girl under ten at £30 a year, double her Lowood salary. She gets her references from the school committee and her new place is secured. As she waits for the carrier to collect her trunk Bessie arrives. Bessie tells Jane what has been happening at Gateshead and says that seven years ago a Mr Eyre, Jane's uncle, had visited the hall looking for her, but had had to go abroad on business. The next day, Jane leaves for her new job.

After the dramatic conclusion of the last chapter, here the early part of Jane's life is neatly tied up. She reflects on her time at Lowood, we are reminded of the characters she lived with at Gateshead, and a new character, Mr Eyre, is introduced. Jane is about to enter a new phase of her life. The chapter captures a moment at which Jane suddenly seems to grow psychologically. The use of repetition – 'I desired liberty; for liberty I gasped; for liberty I uttered a prayer' – is demonstrative of Jane's strength of feeling. As she throws off her Lowood training, she suddenly realises that she has the inner resources to escape and 'surmount the blue peaks' that she sees ahead of her.

The heart of the novel lies in Jane's descriptions of what is going on in her own mind and her feelings, especially 'conscience' and 'passion', are often given their own voice. In this instance a 'kind fairy' seems to tell her what to do to get a new situation. These moments of **personification** help us to understand why Jane acts as she does.

stimulus stimulation
watch stay awake
plucked failed exam

CHAPTER 11   Jane arrives at Thornfield Hall

Jane has reached Millcote and the chapter opens as she waits to be met by someone from Thornfield Hall. She finally arrives late at night, and is met by Mrs Fairfax. Mrs Fairfax is very cordial and Jane feels quite comfortable in her new place. The next day she learns that a Mr Rochester is master of the house and that her pupil, Miss Adela Varens, is his ward. Mr Rochester seldom visits the hall, but he is well liked and respected. Jane is shown over the house and while descending from the attic hears an eerie laugh.

By this point Jane Eyre has become an accomplished young lady, as suggested by Bessie in the last chapter, however, as a governess she is nonetheless placed in an awkward social position. In this chapter Jane leaves her childhood and schooling behind her and enters adolescence: 'inexperienced youth'. The opening lines make it clear that we are reading a novel, despite the book's subtitle, 'An Autobiography'. However, because of this clarification we are no longer sure that we know who our narrator is; is it still Jane Eyre or someone else?

Several new characters are introduced – Mrs Fairfax, Adèle Varens, Mr Rochester, Grace Poole – and numerous events are **foreshadowed** It is worth paying close attention to the description of the house and grounds, as there are many close associations between them and their master, Mr Rochester. At the end of the chapter the description of the attic, the reference to an eerie laugh and the allusion to Bluebeard add to the **gothic** tone of the Thornfield section of the text and foreshadow the discovery that Rochester is already married to a madwoman whom he keeps locked away on the third floor.

romantic wild landscape

canzonette short light song

'La Ligue ... Fontaine' one of the animal fables of the French author Jean de la Fontaine

cabinet piano upright piano

spar crystal

Tyrian-dyed coloured a reddish purple

Parian white marble

Hebrew ark with gilt winged cherubs, see Exodus 25, 36, 37, I Kings 6:29–35

"after life's ... well" Shakespeare, *Macbeth* III, 2. 23

Bluebeard's castle reference to fairy story in which a young wife is allowed to enter any room she wants in her husband's castle except one, in which she finds the bodies of his previous wives

syllabic speech-like

CHAPTER 12   **Jane meets her master, Mr Rochester**

Jane settles in. When she is bored she goes for walks or climbs to the attic and longs for excitement. One day she walks to Hay to deliver a letter. It is very cold and as she rests she sees a horse and rider slip on some ice. She helps the man remount his horse and continues on her errand. When she returns to the hall she discovers that the man she helped was her master, Mr Rochester.

Jane's sojourns in the attic help form an imaginative link between Jane Eyre and Mrs Rochester, as in the 'red-room'. If Jane fell victim to her passions she could become as degenerate as her rival. As we can see from her assumption that Rochester's dog is the Gytrash, Jane's imagination is full of fiends, and the fact that she is sensitive to omens becomes particularly important in Vol. III, Chapter 9. The scene in which Jane and Rochester meet for the first time is dramatic and its outcome, when he finds that 'necessity compels me to make you useful', **foreshadows** his ultimate physical dependence on her, Vol. III, Chapter 12.

'Gytrash' huge black, shaggy dog from folklore that appears in churchyards and lonely lanes at dusk. If it looks you in the eye, you are warned of the death of a relative or friend

mask form

'Like heath … away' Thomas Moore, 'Fallen is the throne...' II. 19–20

'too easy chair' Alexander Pope, *Dunciad* IV. 343

CHAPTER 13   **Mr Rochester quizzes Jane about her past**

Thornfield is enlivened by visitors who come to do business with Mr Edward Fairfax Rochester. At the end of the day Jane and Adèle are invited to take tea with the master who interrogates Jane about her history, asks her to play the piano and requires her to show him her sketches.

Mr Rochester is a **Romantic** figure who, in this chapter, is shown to be forceful and independent; in this respect he is in part Jane's *alter ego*. Their convincing and witty banter brings both characters alive. She is as unconventional and strong-minded as he is and can always match him blow for blow in any conversation. Rochester often refers to Jane as a fairy, a sprite and an imp, 'When you came on me in Hay Lane last night, I thought unaccountably of fairy tales,' but he eventually learns that he must respect her as an individual: a marked departure from the literary conventions of the day.

Jane's paintings reflect the **Romantic** preoccupation with extreme, wild landscapes and exotica.

prenomens first and second names

piquant stimulating

'men in green' fairies always wear the colour green

'head and front of his offending' Shakespeare, *Othello* I, 3. 80
'Approach the table' bring the table closer
copies originals
"The likeness ... none" Milton, *Paradise Lost*, II. 666–73
Latmos mountain in Turkey (Besh Parmark), where, in classical legend, the goddess of the moon, Silene, fell in love with Endymion

CHAPTER 14   Mr Rochester and Jane spar with each other

After a few days Jane and Adèle are again called in to spend the evening with Rochester, who gives Adèle a box of toys and a dress. Jane and Edward engage in another sparring conversation, this time about his appearance, their relative social positions and morality.

The chapter begins in a characteristically journalistic style. These descriptive passages draw us into the action, and are often highly suggestive. However, though the language used is simple and direct, and while, as in the last chapter, the dialogue is generally quite convincing and naturalistic, much of the tenor of the conversation that takes place here is evocative of fairy stories like 'The Beauty and the Beast'.

Jane and Rochester's conversations allow us to learn a lot about his character, attitudes and state of mind. The way in which the different characters speak usually reflects their education and station, and with respect to Adèle it is also indicative of her nationality and training. The extensive use of French in the novel adds veracity to Adèle's exchanges with Jane and makes Jane's own accomplishments more tangible.

interlocutrice companion in conversation
nonnett little nun
'bad eminence' Milton, *Paradise Lost*, II. 6

CHAPTER 15   Mr Rochester tells Jane a little of his past and Jane saves him from a fire

Another conversation takes place between Jane and Rochester as they walk in the hall's grounds. This time he tells Jane Adèle's story. That night, Jane lies awake reflecting on their discussion. Jane no longer thinks that Rochester is ugly. Now he brightens up her life. When she goes to investigate a strange noise she discovers that Rochester's bed has been set alight. She puts the fire out. Rochester goes to find the arsonist and on his return Grace Poole's name is mentioned. Rochester prefers to compliment Jane on her actions rather than talk about the fire, however, and before they part he confesses that he feels a natural sympathy for her.

> This chapter forms the end of the first volume and marks a clear alteration in Rochester and Jane's relationship. The fire **foreshadows** the destruction of Thornfield as outlined in Vol. III, Chapter 10 and, with Jane's speculation about Rochester, generates a sense of suspense. Again, Rochester is shown to need Jane who seems to know him better than he knows himself. He seems unable to express himself, and his true feelings are revealed as he begins to lose fluency. We know Jane's hopes and fears because we are given a privileged insight into her innermost thoughts; we know his through conversation and what he does not say.

> **Apollo Belvidere** famous statue of Apollo in the Vatican
> **hotel** town house
> **dentelles** lace
> **spoonie** demonstratively fond lover
> **'Job's leviathan...habergeon'** Job 41:26
> **'heart's core'** Shakespeare, *Hamlet* III, 2. 73
> **extinguisher** of candle
> **chicken in the pip** diseased chicken
> **Beulah** an idyllic place, see Isaiah 62:4 and Bunyan, *The Pilgrim's Progress*

VOLUME II

CHAPTER 1   **Jane tries to come to her senses**

The next morning Jane sees Grace Poole, the suspected arsonist, helping to restore Rochester's room. When Jane confronts her she warns Jane to keep her door locked at night. Jane is puzzled by this and hopes to ask Rochester about it. At tea-time she finds out that he has gone away to visit some fine friends. Mrs Fairfax describes some of the people he will meet and Jane realises that she has been foolish in thinking she could be one of his favourites. She paints a self-portrait called 'Portrait of a Governess, disconnected, poor, and plain'.

> At the opening of Volume II, the suspense generated in the previous chapter is maintained while our curiosity is aroused by Jane's strange conversation with Grace. No-one is quite what they seem. Events in Vol. II, Chapter 10 are **foreshadowed** when Grace warns Jane to lock her door. It becomes clear that Jane is falling in love with Rochester, and her method of handling him once they are engaged is suggested here in her cocksure pleasure at 'vexing and soothing him'. Several new characters are introduced and help highlight Jane's ambiguous social position. As suggested by the title she gives to her portrait, she cannot realistically hope to marry Rochester. Rochester will use Blanche Ingram to make Jane jealous.

momentarily moment by moment
unvarnished tale Shakespeare, *Othello*, I, 3. 90

CHAPTER 2   Miss Ingram and friends visit Thornfield

After a fortnight the party comes to stay at Thornfield. The house is prepared, extra servants are got in. During the preparations, Jane overhears part of a conversation about Grace Poole, but cannot make much sense of it as she is deliberately excluded from the mystery. The fine people soon arrive, the house is full of guests, servants, hustle and bustle. The next day, Jane and Adèle are invited to join the party after dinner. As the ladies chatter, as the men enter and as all engage in the evening's amusement, Jane watches. While she does so she overhears a nasty conversation about governesses. When Jane slips away Rochester comes after her and insists that she join the party in the drawing room every evening until they go.

> The whole of this chapter repays close analysis, for example, what does Rochester want to say when he hesitates: 'Good-night, my —'? Jane's hatred of company was **foreshadowed** in Vol. I, Chapter 4 but in this instance we are provided with a slice of upper-class life, as observed by someone who sees herself as a social outcast. Again, the

fact that Jane is in a socially anomalous position is important and adds piquancy to the conversation about governesses.

The frequent use of the present tense gives Jane's descriptions immediacy and draws us into the scene. However, because Jane's narrative is written some years after the event she can also reflect more maturely and quite humorously on her adolescent attempts to 'master' herself and dismiss her highly inappropriate feelings. Irony clearly plays an important part in the whole of the novel. Incidentally, Jane constantly refers to Rochester as her 'master' in a way which suggests that he in fact psychologically 'masters' her.

'a very pleasant ... trouble' Psalms 46:1

Mesrour Executioner

'Some natural tears she shed' Milton, *Paradise Lost*, XII. 645

'minois chiffonné' with charming irregularity

Dowager lives independently on her dead husband's property

'in the pip' bad tempered

quiz tease

Rizzio ... Mary David Rizzio, Italian singer, Mary Queen of Scots' secretary and lover

black Bothwell ... James Hepburn Earl of Bothwell who murdered Mary Queen of Scots' first husband in order to marry her

Corsairs Byron, *The Corsairs* (1814). Some confusion exists as to the date at which the novel is set

CHAPTER 3   A game of charades, a stranger and a gypsy

The party stays on and engages in a variety of pastimes, including a game of charades. Jane is convinced that Rochester will marry Miss Ingram, 'for interest and connexions'. While Rochester is absent a stranger, Mr Mason, calls to see him. While he waits for Rochester's return an old gypsy woman appears and insists on telling 'the gentry their fortunes'. Eventually, all of the ladies go to her, including Jane.

The stress of the chapter lies on appearances. The stage-like entrances and exits of the last chapter are played on in the game of charades, and in the dramatic arrival of the stranger and old gypsy woman. Jane's reflections on social convention and the necessity of marrying for love are important when she comes to consider St John Rivers's proposal in Volume III. More significantly, though, a marriage founded on charade – Rochester seems to specialise in mock marriages – and the arrival of a stranger are distinctly ominous.

sacques, modes, lappets all eighteenth-century items of women's dress
pantomimes mime or silent play acting
Paynim pagan
bowstring used by assassins
'She hasted ... to drink' Genesis 24
Bridewell London prison
old Mother Bunches Mother Bunch was a byword for jests and 'old wives' tales'
crock (dialect) smut
tinkler tinker
the old gentleman the devil
Sibyl female prophet
'I'm sure ... not right' Goldsmith, *Vicar of Wakefield*

CHAPTER 4   Jane and the gypsy

Jane meets the gypsy who seems bent on asking her questions, rather than telling her fortune, which makes Jane suspicious. The gypsy reads Jane's face then asks her to go. Jane hesitates and realises that the gypsy is actually Mr Rochester. When he hears that Mr Mason has arrived in his absence he is stunned, but when everyone retires all seems well.

Jane and the gypsy's conversation begins in a way that is again reminiscent of 'Little Red Riding hood': this mirrors Jane's conversation with Mr Brocklehurst in Vol. I, Chapter 4. Contrast the gypsy's assessment of her as 'cold', 'sick' and 'silly' with her own insistence that she is 'disconnected, poor, and plain'. The unveiling of Mr Rochester is dramatically and symbolically significant, further developing the motif of charade. With the arrival of Mr Mason, we move closer to the mystery at the heart of Thornfield.

'nickered' laughed
blackaviced dark-skinned
'The passions may rage ... things' Psalms, 2:1
'Strong wind ... voice' I Kings 19:11–12

"the play is played out" untraced quotation
'Did I dream ... still?' Keats, 'Ode to a Nightingale' II. 79–80
eld old
"Off, ye lendings!" Shakespeare, *King Lear* III, 4. 111

CHAPTER 5   The company are woken by a scream and Jane nurses Mr Mason

Jane hears a cry, struggle and a call for help. Once he has pacified his guests, Rochester asks Jane to follow him into the attic and leaves her to nurse Mr Mason who has been slashed by a knife. She and Mr Mason are sworn to silence while Rochester fetches a surgeon and while she waits Jane speculates about what has happened. As dawn comes Rochester returns and the doctor quickly dresses Mason's wounds. He is spirited away and Jane is left puzzling over events but Rochester begins one of his moral conversations. Finally he starts talking about marrying Miss Ingram.

> The bloody mystery deepens. Because Jane is unable to follow any of the conversations that take place around her or what Rochester says to her, neither can we. The hall, which is always symbolically important, becomes more mysterious, more **gothic**. Notice how Thornfield and its owner, who still seems to be playing charades, are linked.
>
> Jane is morally direct and sure-footed; she will only 'obey' Rochester if it is right to do so and this becomes important at the end of the volume. The full moon is clearly associated with the lunatic antics of Mrs Rochester, who behaves like a vampire – picked up again in Vol. II, Chapter 10. Miss Ingram is described as 'a real strapper ... big, brown and buxom' in other words she looks just like Mrs Rochester, whose room is directly above Jane's, and in many respects also behaves like Bertha before Edward married her.

curtain bed curtain
mystic mysterious, strange
outraged attacked
glamour enchantment
'your sun at noon ... eclipse' Milton, *Samson Agonistes* II. 80–81
Carthage in St Augustine's *Confessions* a city of debauchery

CHAPTER 6   Jane dreams about a baby every night for a week

Jane is unsettled by a recurring dream about an infant and sees it as a bad
omen. She is summoned to Gateshead by her aunt who is very ill. Her
cousin John has died in mysterious circumstances. Rochester is reluctant to
let her go, but she finally gets a leave of absence. While talking to Rochester
she asks him to find her another situation before he marries. Her arrival at
Gateshead brings back memories; she is welcomed by Bessie though Miss
Eliza and Miss Georgiana are less agreeable. Jane insists on seeing her aunt
who is very confused. Some days later her aunt gives her a three-year-old
letter from a John Eyre, her uncle, who wanted to adopt her. Jane refers to
Mrs Reed as 'aunt', but despite Jane's attempts at kindness there can be no
reconciliation. Mrs Reed dies.

> The chapter begins in reflective mood and moves on into the
> structure of 'The Beauty and the Beast'. We are filled in on the recent
> history of the Reeds which provides a link back to Vol. I and allows
> Jane to complete the business of her childhood. Her aunt's use of the
> third person allows us to gain some understanding of Mrs Reed's
> point of view. Jane tries to behave as Helen Burns would have
> done, but learns that she must be true to herself and that people do
> not change in the way her religious schooling suggests that they
> should.
>
> Jane's cousins represent two opposing kinds of conventional
> femininity, the kind whose sole aim is to marry to advantage, the
> other self-sacrificing and inclined to retreat from the world onto the
> moral high ground. Notice how Jane detests all things that smack of
> popish Catholicism, as opposed to good English Protestantism. Jane
> is a chauvinist. Her uncle becomes important in Vol. II, Chapter 11
> and Vol. III, Chapter 7.
>
> The reference at the beginning of the chapter to 'presentiments',
> 'sympathies' and 'signs' becomes particularly pertinent in Vol. III,
> Chapter 9, but Jane's sensitivity to all kinds of omens is often used to
> **foreshadow** coming events and helps drive the plot, add **irony** and
> create suspense. Uncanny imagery and symbolism help pull the
> different parts of the novel together into an organic whole.

reprobation damnation
Cairngorm semi-precious stone
'quiz' a puzzling eccentric
'the Rubric' specify how Anglican church services should be conducted
husky dry
traits features

CHAPTER 7   **Jane realises that Thornfield and its master together make up 'home'**

A month later Jane leaves Gateshead. Georgiana eventually marries and Eliza finally takes the veil. When she returns to Thornfield, Jane is surprised by her feelings for Rochester and discloses that she would not really like to leave him again. There is a rumour that he is about to marry, but few preparations.

A short interim chapter in which several loose ends are tied up. Jane returns to Thornfield which reappears under its pleasantest aspect and at the beginning of summer, an appropriate time and setting for courtship.

The use of the present tense, as Jane approaches Thornfield Hall, gives the whole scene immediacy.

second-sight ability to tell the future

CHAPTER 8   **Rochester proposes**

Jane meets Rochester as she walks in the grounds on Midsummer eve, and he engages her in conversation. He says that she must leave Thornfield as he will soon marry. She begins to cry. They sit under the old chestnut tree and he suddenly confesses that he has no intention of marrying Miss Ingram at all, he actually wants to marry Jane. Jane doubts and quizzes, but finally accepts him. During the night a great storm splits the old chestnut tree in two.

This provides us with the first climax of the novel. The setting is Edenic and includes allusions to Wordsworth as well as Shakespeare's *A Midsummer Night's Dream*, a play in which lovers are constantly tricked, turned around and bewitched by fairies. The language is heightened and passionate, the tone one of foreboding.

Throughout the novel Thornfield and its grounds are closely associated with their master and the fact that the old tree is split in two is ominous, given that the tree is symbolic of Jane and Rochester's relationship. The storm also suggests that God will not pardon Rochester or sanction his actions – he is still in effect living a lie even though the charade of an engagement with Miss Ingram is over.

'Day its fervid ... wasted' Thomas Campbell, 'The Turkish Lady' l.5
lady-clock (dialect) lady-bird; (children's rhyme) 'Lady-bird, lady-bird fly away home, / Your house is on fire, / Your children all flown'
'morsel of bread, living water' (biblical) refers to communion ceremony

CHAPTER 9   **Arrangements are made for the wedding**

The next day Rochester says that they will be married in a month. He wants to shower Jane with gifts and take her on a tour of Europe. Jane is wary and does not want to be flattered or dressed in jewels. Mrs Fairfax is not entirely easy about what has happened and is worried that something will go wrong. Jane, Adèle and Rochester go to Millcote where Jane and Rochester tussle over dresses and jewels. Jane determines to write to her uncle in order to secure her independence and she insists that she continue as governess for the month of their engagement. That evening she gets him to sing to her and she consistently keeps him at arm's length during the rest of their courtship.

The fact that there is trouble ahead is clearly **foreshadowed**, which adds suspense to what is otherwise a straightforward romance. The fact that the narrator can drop hints that Rochester is still hiding something – 'as if well pleased at seeing a danger averted' – and the fact that Jane can ignore them can make us feel a little uncomfortable until we remember that the narrative is being told by an older and wiser Jane some time after the event.

Rochester takes up Jane's psychological usage of 'master' when he says 'you master me'. Also notice the explicit reference to Samson's story, which is referred to obliquely several times in the rest of the novel. Later, St John comments that Jane is 'original' in a similar way to Rochester in Vol. III, Chapter 6 and it is worth remembering her joke

with Rochester about becoming a missionary when St John Rivers's
plans for her are revealed.

mustard-seed fairy in *A Midsummer Night's Dream*
Hercules in classical legend Hercules is enslaved by his love for Omphale
Samson Samson reveals the secret of his strength to Delilah, his mistress
"gild refined gold" *King John* IV, 2. 11
Ashasuerus Persian king who marries a poor Jewish girl, Esther
'I lay ... soul' Shakespeare, *Hamlet* III, 4. 145
'the world ... lost' Dryden, *All for Love, or the World well Lost*
Danae in classical legend, Danae is seduced by Zeus who appears as a shower
of gold
three-tailed bashaw Turkish ruler
'Yes, bonny ... tyne' Burns, 'The bonny wee thing', 11. 3–4
The truest love ... loved am I the song is Brontë's

CHAPTER 10   Jane sees a spectre

As Jane waits for Rochester's return from business she is disturbed by an
event that happened the previous night. As she walks in the grounds she
passes by the old chestnut tree. Eventually, Rochester arrives and, at
midnight, she tells him that the previous night an apparition came to her
room, and tore the veil he had given her. Rochester assures her that she
merely saw Grace Poole, and sends her to sleep with Adèle in the nursery.

A **gothic** chapter, full of foreboding. Notice the motif of the little
child and her dream that Thornfield is reduced to a shell as examples
of prescience. Jane's thoughts on contemplating the ruin of the
chestnut tree **foreshadow** her feelings when reunited with Rochester
at the end of the novel. There is **irony** in her refusal to use the luggage
labels because 'Mrs Rochester' does not yet exist, especially when Mrs
Rochester tears Jane's own veil. There are also references to earlier
events in the novel, particularly in the red-room and Bertha's attack
on Mr Mason.

D.V. God willing
portmanteau clothes-hanger
hypochondria anxiety or depression
'events ... mine' Romans 8:28

'wilderness ... like a rose' Isaiah 35:1
blonde silk lace
"with a sullen moaning sound" Scott, *The Lay of the Last Minstrel*, I.13.1
Vampyre (German spelling) vampire

CHAPTER 11   Jane discovers that Rochester is already married

Jane dresses for church and Rochester hurries her on to the ceremony. The service begins, but as the clergyman asks if there is any impediment a man steps forward to declare that Rochester is already married, to one Bertha Antoinette Mason. The stranger is a solicitor and he is accompanied by Mr Mason, Mrs Rochester's brother. Rochester admits that he has attempted bigamy and takes the church party into the house where they can meet his wife. Bertha is revealed to be a madwoman kept under lock and key, under the care of Grace Poole. Mr Mason intervened because of Jane's letter to her uncle, Mason's employee. Jane retreats to her room.

The bad omens of the last few chapters are fulfilled. Thornfield and its master's mysteries are revealed. This is the last chapter of Volume II and serves to tie up several loose ends. We are left wondering what Jane will do next.

a Creole a native West Indian of any race
'quenchless fire and deathless worm' imagery taken from Mark 9:43–8 and Matthew 5:29
ragout a mixture
'with what ... judged' Matthew 7:2
'Funchal correspondent of his house' representative of the Mason firm in Funchal, capital city of Madeira
'decline' consumption
a subtle ... Egypt Exodus 12:23–30
'Be not far ... help' Psalms 22:11
'the waters ... overflowed me' Psalms 69:2

VOLUME III

CHAPTER 1   Jane leaves Thornfield

Next morning Jane's conscience tells her that she must leave her master. She is able to forgive Rochester, but though he tells Jane Bertha Mason's history she still refuses to become his mistress. That night Jane slips out, wanders over the fields and finally catches a coach that will take her away from the hall.

> The chapter of heightened emotion is the last in the Thornfield section and repays close analysis. It opens with an example of **personification** in which Jane looks to her Lowood training and follows 'Conscience' not 'Passion'. Notice how, feeling alone and unloved as she did in childhood, she recalls the red-room at Gateshead. Her tolerance *in extremis* she draws on her schooling to provide her with inner strength.
>
> The bulk of the chapter consists of Rochester's narrative, through which we learn more about his character, how he has matured and his current state of mind. In contrast, the brief, journalistic style in which Jane's mental ordeal is described is striking. Symbolically the moon is an important motif, while the dawn chorus that greets Jane as she leaves Thornfield reminds us of her reflections on the old chestnut tree in the hall's grounds.
>
> Brontë once again addresses the reader directly at a time of crisis: 'Reader! – I forgave him ...'.
>
> **'pluck out ... transfix it'** Matthew 5:28–30
> **'one little ewe lamb ... bosom'** II Samuel 12:3
> **'tent of Achan'** Joshua 7
> **upas tree** a poisonous tree fabled to give off a putrid steam
> **Grimsby Retreat** fictional mental asylum
> **'Samson's ... tow'** Judges 16:9
> **intemperate** drinks alcohol excessively
> **Messalina** a woman with a heightened sexual appetite, originally simply the wife of the Emperor Claudius

CHAPTER 2   Jane is taken in by the Rivers family

The coach leaves Jane at Whitcross, a crossroads in the middle of the moors. She sleeps in a secluded spot and the next day sets out to look for work. She has no luck and is forced to beg. She sleeps in a wood and the next day again fails to find work.

Finally, Jane walks back into the moors and discovers an isolated farmhouse. She sees an old woman, Hannah, and two young ladies, Diana and Mary, knitting and reading in the kitchen. Jane knocks but the servant refuses to help her, but just as the door is shut in her face the master, Mr St John Rivers, returns and takes her in.

> Jane's nature will not allow her to accept her fate passively. This chapter is full of **pathos**. The language is direct, unsentimental, and gives a very clear sense of the utter psychological and physical desolation that Jane feels at this point. This is made more poignant by the scene of perfect domesticity that greets her in her last desperate moments.
>
> **'my Maker ... of me'** Luke 12:20
> **'"Da trat hervor ... Grimms"'** quotations from Schiller, *The Robbers*, V.1
> **'the anchor of hope ... gone'** draws on Hebrews 6:19
> **'If I were a masterless ... tonight'** Shakespeare, *King Lear* IV, 7. 35–7

CHAPTER 3   Jane recovers

Jane lies ill for three days but gradually recovers. When she gets up she helps the servant, Hannah, and finds out more about the Rivers family. Old Mr Rivers has just died and St John, Mary and Diana have come home to sort out his affairs. The young ladies have been working as governesses, while St John is the clergyman of the hamlet, Morton, where Jane went begging. When the family return from a walk they quiz Jane about her circumstances and history. She refuses to tell them much, but does explain that she was mostly recently a governess. She asks to be called Jane Elliott, but admits that it is not her real name. They agree to let her stay with them until she can find some kind of employment.

> When Jane rises she begins a new phase of her life. This is a discreetly **expository** chapter in which we begin to learn something about the

Rivers family. The two sisters and their brother are shown to be the mirror images of the Reeds. Jane's inherent snobbery is revealed in her conversation with Hannah, the servant, whose English Jane involuntarily corrects.

Brontë is critical of religion which exists only in the mind: 'If you are a Christian, you ought not to consider poverty a crime'.

'day of small things' Zechariah 4:10

plain-work-woman woman who does plain sewing

CHAPTER 4   **Jane lives happily with the Rivers and regains her health**

Jane is very happy living with the Rivers sisters who coincide with her exactly in their tastes, conversation and interests. St John remains a remote figure, but he eventually asks her to become schoolmistress at Morton. She accepts, even though she will only teach the local cottage girls, as it will allow her to become independent. She also learns that the Rivers's uncle has just died and, due to a quarrel with their father, has left them out of his will. Shortly after this the family go their separate ways.

Though St John Rivers is an Evangelical clergyman he is shown to be the moral opposite of Mr Brocklehurst. Equally, compared to Rochester, St John is hard, cold, and absolutely self-controlled. St John is quite a frightening character who can clearly overpower Jane, but she can still step back and criticise his want of human affection, which is something she craves.

enthusiasm fanaticism

nervous tense and energetic

election individual salvation

peace ... understanding Philippians 4:7

eligible desirable

church militant role of church as the conquest of evil

"Rise, follow me!" see the Gospels

ideal imaginative, opposite of material

cyphering arithmetic

'my nature ... useless' Milton, 'When I consider ...'

CHAPTER 5   Jane becomes a schoolmistress

Jane takes up her position as schoolmistress. As she sits in her cottage on the first evening she reflects on her actions in leaving Rochester and feels that she was right to leave him, but nonetheless is very sad. St John visits her and explains that he hopes to becomes a missionary. While they talk a young lady, Miss Rosamond Oliver, the school's benefactress, arrives. There is an obvious mutual attraction between her and St John, though St John is careful not to show any expression of it.

> The parallels between St John and Brocklehurst continue; both men would hope to 'turn the bent of nature'. Miss Oliver and St John are, physically, perfectly matched, like Rochester and Jane. However, St John, unlike Rochester, seems determined to turn away from love and, like Helen Burns, sacrifice himself to a death-dealing faith.

The air ... balm Walter Scott, *The Lay of the Last Minstrel* III.14.3–4
Lot's wife Genesis 19:26
Peri beautiful good fairy

CHAPTER 6   St John steals a piece of paper

Jane settles in at the school and becomes well-liked locally, but still tends to have disturbing dreams. Miss Oliver often visits the school, when St John is teaching, and goes to the cottage when Jane is at home. Jane meets Mr Oliver and is invited to the hall where he tells her more about the Rivers family. Jane sketches Rosamond and St John appears one evening while she is working on the picture. Jane takes the opportunity to find out how he feels about Miss Oliver. As he leaves he tears and takes away a small strip of paper.

> Jane's dreams provide us with a very real picture of female desire and are notable for their psychological truth. Despite her apparent self-control, Jane is still struggling with her palpable need for Rochester. The references to Rochester in the Morton section of the novel serve to link this with the Thornfield chapters and help point up the contrast between her two suitors.
>
> St John is, as he says, 'a cold, hard, ambitious man', determined to reject life in order to build 'a mansion in heaven'. Jane cannot

understand this, but, as with Helen Burns, she can admire him. If Rochester is all feeling, St John is all reason.

"sitting in sunshine ... sweet" Thomas Moore, *Lalla Rookh*, Third Day

taken an amiable caprice taken a liking

lusus naturae (Latin) freak of nature

a new publication though Brontë says this is Scott's *Marmion* (1808), this does not agree with any of the other references to the date at which the novel is set (generally 1820–30s)

'burst' ... 'the silent sea' Coleridge, *The Rime of the Ancient Mariner* II. 101–2

'blood-bleached robe' Revelation 7:14

deistic accepts that God exists

"till this mortal ... immortality" I Corinthians 15:53

'Cui bono' (Latin) for whose sake?

CHAPTER 7   Jane inherits a fortune and gains a family

When St John suddenly appears the next night it is to bring Jane news. He recounts her own story and tells her that the slip of paper he took the day before confirmed her as one 'Jane Eyre' whose uncle has died and left her £20,000. She also discovers that this man is the uncle who refused to leave a penny to the Rivers family. Jane is an heiress and has a family. She decides to divide the fortune among them all.

> Finally, Jane's fairytale begins to come true. This is one of the most deliberately fantastical elements in the story, as highlighted by the fact that it takes place at Christmas, but each piece of the puzzle has been subtly introduced earlier in the novel.
>
> Jane has longed for a real home and family since the outset of the novel. She has also often frequently wished to have status and to be independent, see for example, Vol. II, Chapter 9. The uncle in Madeira was introduced when she returned to Gateshead, in Vol. II, Chapter 6, while the difficult relationships between the Rivers, Eyres and Reeds have been hinted at throughout.

CHAPTER 8   St John proposes

Jane shuts up the school for Christmas and goes back to Moor House where she and Hannah spruce the place up. Diana and Mary return to enjoy the holiday. St John tells them that he is determined to leave England and that Miss Oliver is to marry a Mr Granby. Jane is, as she hoped, treated like a sister by Diana and Mary, but St John remains reserved. He insists that she travel to the school in all weathers, and asks her to learn Hindustani. One night he kisses her on the cheek.

Jane wants to know what has become of Rochester and writes two letters to Mrs Fairfax, but as both remain unanswered her hopes die. In the summer, St John proposes; he wants a missionary's wife and thinks that Jane will be perfect. She refuses to marry him, though she says she would accompany him to India as his sister. He will not accept this offer and they argue. After they finally shake hands, they part coolly.

Jane finally has a real home to return to, something she puzzled over in Vol. II, Chapter 7, but she cannot imagine St John succumbing to domesticity and she shrinks in horror at the idea of being his wife. The struggle that now begins to take place between them is what finally brings her to maturity.

Jane's admiration for St John is always tempered by bleakness. She sees through his high-minded ideals, but despite this he slowly begins to overwhelm her. Her passionate nature is gradually frozen over by his kisses and her subsequent observation in the next chapter that his love would kill her seems absolutely true.

paysannes and Bauerinnen French and German peasants
'turning to profit ... account' Matthew 25:14–30
'confusion worse confounded' *Paradise Lost* II.996
Caffre Kaffir
unlikely (dialect) unsuitable
'When he said ... did it' Matthew 8:9
a visionary messenger ... help us!' Acts 16:9–10
'chiefest of sinners' I Timothy 1:15
'the vice of Demas' II Timothy 4:10
'put your hand to the plough' Luke 9:62
'have denied ... infidels' I Timothy 5:8
'Looked ... hill' Scott, *The Lay of the Last Minstrel* V.26.1

CHAPTER 9   St John repeats his proposal, but Jane hears Rochester
             calling to her

St John continues to treat Jane coolly and refuses to respond to her
overtures of friendship. They fight again and when he leaves the house she
explains what is going on to Diana. That evening, after prayers, he proposes
again and she nearly succumbs. Once more *in extremis* she begs God for
help and suddenly hears Rochester's voice calling out to her.

> The application of principle is shown to be worse than malice and this
> radical departure from the conventions of nineteenth-century
> literature led to widespread criticism of the novel when it was first
> published. Here we see an admixture of the real and the fantastic as
> the chapter moves from the psychological to the clairvoyant –
> corresponding to Rochester's own experience (see next chapter).
>
> Jane sees through St John to 'the corrupt man within him'. He is
> absolutely brutal in the execution of his faith and like Brocklehurst he
> is determined to bend Jane to his will, to kill her true self. Where
> Brocklehurst was a black pillar, St John is ice-cold white marble.
>
> The sheer power of St John's personality is quite terrifying and Jane's
> ultimate struggle with him is just as dramatic as her battle with
> Rochester in Chapter 1. As she says 'I was almost as hard beset by him
> now as I had been once before, in a different way, by another.'
>
> St John and Rochester symbolise the conflict between Reason and
> Feeling in Jane's character. Suddenly, she transcends this conflict,
> realises that to be herself, in order to live, she must follow her nature:
> 'It was *my* time to assume ascendancy. *My* powers were in play and in
> force.'
>
> **'the duty of man … times'** Matthew 18:21–2
> **'become a castaway'** I Corinthians 9:27
> **'God sees not as man sees'** I Samuel 16:7
> **a brand snatched from the burning** Amos 4:11, Zechariah 3:2
> **'bid to work … "shall work"'** John 9:4
> **'the fate of Dives … life'** Luke 16:19–31
> **'that better part … from you'** Luke 10:42
> **'rolled together like a scroll'** Isaiah 34:4

CHAPTER 10   Jane returns to Thornfield

The next day Jane catches the coach to Thornfield and sets out for the hall across the fields. When she reaches it she sees nothing but a shell. On asking at The Rochester Arms she discovers that there has been a fire, that Bertha is dead and that Mr Rochester is alive but was maimed when he tried to save her. He is now living at Ferndean and Jane organises a carriage to take her there.

> As we reach the **denouement** so the tension mounts. Jane's departure from Morton echoes her flight from Thornfield; now she is absolutely sure of herself and her actions, though she has no way of guessing the consequences. She has become a mature woman who knows her own mind and can resist convention.
>
> Her dream, in Vol. II, Chapter 10, foretold that the hall would be burnt down. Rochester's withdrawal to Ferndean and the happy life they end up leading there is a little odd given what he says about it in Vol. III, Chapter 1 and Jane's subsequent description.
>
> **'watch and pray ... weak'** Matthew 36:41, Mark 14:38
> **like the earthquake ... aghast** Acts 16:26–9
> **tideless sea of the south** Mediterranean

CHAPTER 11   Jane arrives at Ferndean

Jane reaches Ferndean as night falls and sees Rochester in the yard. She goes in and introduces herself to John and Mary, the servants, then takes Rochester candles and a glass of water, pretending to be the maid. Their reunion is emotional and joyful. They eat supper together and the next morning she explains what she has been doing. Eventually he proposes for the second time and she accepts.

> This is a magical chapter in which Jane and Rochester slip easily into their old ways – she teases him for a while to make him jealous then soothes him again – but in which they are both altered. Jane and Rochester have both matured; Rochester has learnt to respect Jane – his realisation at their initial meeting that 'I must be aided, and by that hand' comes true – while she has learnt to serve, but also to act according to her nature. The language is fluid, the conversation natural.

sightless Samson Samson's eyes are put out when he is finally betrayed: Judges 16:21

lameter cripple

'a "faux air" of Nebuchadnezzar in the fields' Daniel 4:33

'to leave my tale half-told' this is what Scheherazade does in order to avoid execution in the *Arabian Nights*

'If Saul ... harp' I Samuel 16:23

redd (dialect) tidied

'The rain is over and gone' Song of Solomon 2:11

highlows boot

Vulcan blacksmith, from Homer

scrag neck

'valley of the shadow of death' Psalms 23:4

'I kept ... in my heart' Luke 2:19

CHAPTER 12   Jane marries Rochester

Jane and Rochester marry quietly. She writes to Mary, Diana and St John; later, Diana and Mary marry. She visits Adèle and moves her from one school to another; over time the girl grows up into a pleasant young lady. Jane and Rochester are very happy together; his sight partially recovers and they have a son. St John Rivers never marries; at the close of the novel he is waiting to die in India.

In this final chapter various loose ends are tied up. Rochester and Jane have established a relationship based on mutual dependence. However, it is worth noting that Jane says 'Reader, I married him', not 'we were married'. Also, the novel does not end with Jane's description of her married bliss, but with St John's imminent death.

'who live without God ... things' Philippians 3:19

bone of ... flesh Genesis 2:23

Greatheart character from Bunyan's *The Pilgrim's Progress*, who escorts women and children

'without fault ... God' Revelation 14:5

'incorruptible crown' I Corinthians 9:25

'good and faithful servant' Matthew 25:21

'His own words ... this' Revelation 22:20

PART THREE

CRITICAL APPROACHES

CHARACTERISATION

JANE EYRE

Jane Eyre is essentially a young woman who is trying to grow up in a society that does not value her or her skills, and as such carries the theme of the novel. She is an advocate for her sex, and asserts herself, liberates herself and makes herself happy because she believes she has a right to be so. Jane is a credible and realistic character and it is therefore all too easy to treat her as a real person who has an independent existence beyond the text. We get to know her innermost thoughts and deepest feelings through the course of the novel; in fact the heart of the novel actually lies in Jane's descriptions of what is going on in her own mind, and we are therefore drawn into a very close relationship with her. However, Jane is also Cinderella-like, or like the heroine of 'The Beauty and the Beast', though unlike these fairytale characters Jane is plain both as a child and as an adult. As Mr Rochester's servants comment at Ferndean in the Conclusion, 'she ben't one o' th' handsomest'.

Jane is born poor, is soon orphaned and lives out her childhood with her Aunt Reed and three cousins who detest and bully her. Unlike Cinderella she does not have to work as a servant, but her life at Gateshead and then at Lowood school is one of drudgery. Even when she becomes a governess she is still placed in an awkward social position, because at the time governesses were a social anomaly. Neither servants nor members of their employer's family, governesses had to be respectable young ladies when respectable young ladies were not supposed to work for their living. Jane's prospects finally pick up, however, when she discovers that she has an alternative set of cousins who will treat her as an equal and when, rather than a fairy godmother, her rich uncle finally leaves her enough money to become independent. Eventually, she marries her very own handsome 'prince', Mr Rochester, and the novel ends 'My Edward and I are happy'. It is, therefore, the complex psychic development that Jane undergoes and the everyday setting of the novel that manage to make her such an impressive character, rather than her somewhat implausible story.

Jane dominates and controls the narrative – incidentally, remember that a first-person narrator is not the author – and her reactions and feelings always form the focus of attention, even when another character is talking about him or herself. And because we are privy to her innermost thoughts, we generally take her to be a reliable observer. But it is important to remember here that Jane is narrating events ten years after they have happened. Though she is a child at Gateshead, she tells us about this period as a mature woman, and she herself reminds us of this.

Jane is not a wholly sympathetic figure, either, for example, as we see in Vol. I, Chapter 3, she is quite a precocious child. She is middle class by birth and though impoverished herself she has to learn that the poor are not just an amorphous mass. She can therefore be quite a snob. As an adult, she is also thoroughly imbued with the idea that everything foreign is intrinsically unhealthy and immoral. She makes sure that little Adèle learns to be English, or at least as English as possible, given that she is a French Catholic, and she assumes that the Indian climate will kill her. These are the attitudes of her time and of her class.

At the beginning of the novel Jane is angry, rebellious and hungry for adventure, but as she grows up she learns how to temper her wilder passions so that, unlike many characters in Victorian novels, she is not destroyed by them. Her feelings, especially 'conscience' and 'passion', are often given voices of their own when she is suffering some particular anguish and these moments of **personification** help us to understand why she acts as she does. Torn throughout the novel between her true nature and social convention, in the end she is able to resolve this inherent division by marrying for duty and for love. Yet that victory is one that only she can achieve by force of will and the sacrifice of the characters who are closest to her.

Mr ROCHESTER AND ST JOHN RIVERS

Mr Rochester's growth is important to the unfolding of the plot but, as a secondary character, he is slightly less convincing than Jane Eyre. His story is one of sin and redemption and he is a **Romantic** figure who is well-bred, with brooding, rugged good looks, and combines masculine strength with tenderness. Forceful, passionate and independent, he is determined to have Jane, either as his wife or as his mistress, whatever the cost, yet he is not selfish. We do not generally know his innermost thoughts because Jane does not know them, but we learn a lot about him from his conversations with her; their witty banter brings both characters alive.

Rochester never tries to woo Jane on bended knee; he does not idealise her and she can always match him blow for blow when they argue. Rochester often refers to Jane as a bird, fairy, a sprite and an imp, and he toys with her, hoping to make her jealous, but he eventually learns that he must depend on, respect and see her as an individual if he is to win her hand. This outcome is **foreshadowed** by their first meeting, when his horse falls in the road and he has to lean on her in order to get home. In the end, his dependence on her is made absolute by his blindness, at which point she loves him more than when he simply tried to protect her or shower her with gifts.

The courtship scenes present us with a remarkable departure from literary convention. Through them we see the development of mutual respect between the two major characters; Rochester and Jane's relationship is one that eventually results in a marriage of equals. As Jane says in the final chapter of the novel: 'To be together is for us to be at once as free as in solitude, as gay as in company. To talk to each other is but a more animated and audible thinking'. However, the happy ever after is only made possible because Rochester has been clipped, tamed and chained like an eagle. His disability enables Jane to combine passion with duty. The price of Jane Eyre's happiness is therefore Edward Rochester's sight and right hand.

Rochester is not simply a realistic character, however, he is also symbolic of the part of Jane that is fiery and passionate, rather than icy and self-controlled, and as such he is St John Rivers's opposite. They look like opposites and they act as foils to each other. Rochester is heavy and dark, whereas St John is handsome and fair; Rochester is a man of passion and fire, whereas St John is ambitious, hard and cold. Where Rochester brings Jane alive, she finds St John's passion quite deadly.

St John Rivers is not a sympathetic character, unlike Rochester, but he is still fairly reliable – he is quite honest about his limitations – and convincing. St John, a strict clergyman, lives up to the principles espoused by the Evangelical school proprietor, Mr Brocklehurst; St John is 'marble'

(Volume III, Chapter 8) to Brocklehurst's 'black pillar'. St John is ruthlessly moral and therefore, unlike Brocklehurst, not a hypocrite. St John always acts consistently but unnaturally, as suggested by the fact that he will not follow his nature and marry the woman he loves; his faith, like that of Helen Burns, is one that is death-dealing and grounded in self-sacrifice.

St John therefore symbolises that side of Jane's character which wishes to conform, to obey the rules and suppress her instincts. However, Jane recognises that if she accepts him as her husband she will be crushed, she will lose her identity just as surely as if she had become Rochester's mistress. Both men represent only one half of her and this is why she runs away from St John, back to Thornfield. It is worth noting though that the final passages in the novel are devoted to St John. Like Helen Burns he is about to die in consummation of his faith and this makes Jane cry. His path has led to death, in contrast to her own which has led to life-giving happiness.

Minor characters
Bessie
Jane wins her first moral victory over the nursemaid Bessie who, though she is a relatively minor character, reappears several times – at Lowood and when Jane returns to Gateshead – thus providing a link between the earlier and later parts of the novel. Bessie's ballads and folklore stay with Jane throughout the text, and because Bessie is the only real figure of ordinary, unrefined human kindness in the book she is one of the most sympathetic characters we meet.

The reeds
The Reed family, on the other hand, are utterly detestable. They treat Jane as a nobody, and because we see them entirely from Jane's point of view it is hard to see any good in them. Mrs Reed hates Jane because she has been foisted upon them and Jane's cousins take their lead from their mother. Jane is unhappy and her aunt knows that by treating Jane so badly she is not really obeying her husband's last wish, and Jane always asserts her right to be happy, to be loved above all else. Because of this Mrs Reed feels a certain amount of guilt about Jane; she is tormented by her and this means that she must be expelled from their society. The Reeds show us how Jane is a social outcast and her response to them demonstrates how she blankly

refuses to accept her lot.

THE RIVERS

The Rivers family present us with a mirror image of the Reed family. Unlike the Reeds, the Rivers family offer Jane genuine help when they take her in. Where the two Reed sisters, Eliza and Georgiana, represent two extremes of femininity that are equally despicable, the two Rivers sisters, Diana and Mary, are ideal women and become Jane's role models. Where her cousin John Reed physically abused her, her cousin St John Rivers becomes her teacher.

MR BROCKLEHURST

Just before Jane leaves Gateshead Mrs Reed introduces Jane to the proprietor of Lowood school, Mr Brocklehurst. At Lowood school Jane faces the same treatment as she received at Gateshead, but on a larger scale and in a religious community. Both Gateshead and Lowood work as models of Victorian society, but Brocklehurst in particular represents a form of religious doctrine that Jane instinctively rejects. His faith is all hell-fire and brimstone, he oppresses the children under his care with an extreme Evangelical zeal.

At one point Brocklehurst picks on a girl, Julia Severn, who has curly red hair, simply because he assumes that she must have curled it by artifice. When he is told that her curls are natural he then insists that it be cut off because the children should not conform to nature. While this is going on his own daughters are described as being dressed in fine clothes and wearing their hair according to the latest fashion. This certainly suggests that his religious principles are a mockery of Christianity, that he is a hypocrite who cannot act consistently, but it also suggests that anyone who deviates from the hypocritical standards he sets must be cut out like a canker. He is an example of the men who held power in Victorian Britain and the message is that when men like Brocklehurst hold the reins, then there is no way to live and be yourself; anyone who fails to conform will be pushed out of the way.

HELEN BURNS

When Jane goes to school she is not simply subject to Brocklehurst's rule, however, she also makes friends with Helen Burns who, in sharp contrast to Brocklehurst, represents an ideal of Christian practice. Helen's initial interest in *Rasselas* tells the reader everything he or she needs to know about her. This book argues that only surrender and self-control will enable us to bear with the difficulties of life; Helen endures this world simply because she, like St John, can look forward to the joys of the next. For instance, Helen is picked on by one of the teachers, but always turns the other cheek and, as an ideal woman, meekly resigns herself to her fate.

MISS TEMPLE

When Helen dies of tuberculosis Jane soon rejects this apparently death-dealing vision of self-sacrifice, but quickly falls under the perfect Miss Temple's spell. Miss Temple, Jane's teacher, also has to conform. When she follows her best instincts and gives the children an extra lunch because they have missed breakfast, we are quite clear that she is in the right, but she dare not talk back to Mr Brocklehurst when he upbraids her for her simple kindness. Miss Temple's self-control is a model for Jane until her mentor leaves the school, at which point her influence begins to fade. Through her friendship with these characters Jane learns the sacrifices demanded of women and, once she is beyond their influence, quickly looks for an alternative.

MRS ROCHESTER

One alternative to the ideal of Victorian femininity would be a complete rejection of self-control, as embodied by Mrs Rochester. Bertha is Jane Eyre's *alter ego*, that side of Jane that is driven entirely by passion. She is Rochester's wife, the role promised to Jane, but which she prevents Jane from taking up, as symbolised by her destruction of Jane's veil on the night before the wedding. Jane has some control over her life however, whereas Bertha as a madwoman and an outcast is powerless. A renewed adoption of the values embodied by Helen and Miss Temple therefore allows Jane to escape Bertha's fate. If Jane had followed her heart's desire and stayed with Rochester at this point, she would in a sense have become another Bertha, another madwoman driven purely by her appetites. Luckily, of course,

Bertha's final act means that Jane can ultimately resolve the opposition in herself between passion and self-control.

MISS INGRAM, MISS OLIVER AND MRS FAIRFAX

These three women, because they are simply foils for the other characters, remain relatively two-dimensional and seem in effect to be cast aside once their job is done. Miss Blanche Ingram is described as 'a real strapper … big, brown and buxom' and therefore looks just like Mrs Rochester, and in many respects also behaves like her, before she married Edward. But Rochester simply uses Blanche in order to discover Jane's feelings and once he is done with the heiress we hear no more about her – we do not even know if she finally marries.

Miss Rosamond Oliver, in direct contrast to Jane, is both moneyed and beautiful. An 'earthly angel' she is the perfect match for St John Rivers who loves but spurns her simply because he knows that she would not make a good missionary's wife. This is how we come to realise with Jane that St John is indeed 'hard and cold' (Vol. III, Chapter 10). The last we hear about Rosamond is that she 'is about to be married to Mr Granby, one of the best matches and most estimable residents in S–'. St John sees this as a victory.

Mrs Fairfax, the housekeeper, is a distant relative of Mr Rochester's who, like Jane, is poor but genteel. Where Jane's father was a clergyman, Mrs Fairfax was married to one. She shows Jane, and therefore the reader too, around Thornfield and provides information about the locality and people, including its master. Unlike Jane, however, Mrs Fairfax is not a great observer of character and quickly takes a back seat soon after Jane meets Rochester. Mrs Fairfax then hovers in the background as a moral bystander until Jane leaves Thornfield. When Jane returns we learn that the housekeeper has been sent away to her friends with a handsome annuity.

THEMES

MORAL COURAGE

The central theme of the novel is explored through one young woman's attempt to grow up and gain respect in a society that does not value her or her talents. The problem of being a woman in early Victorian Britain is the

key to our understanding of the text. To begin with, at Gateshead, Jane
learns that moral courage can give her the power to withstand moral
oppression. Because of this she is able to make friends with Bessie and
dominate her surrogate stepmother, Aunt Reed. As she enters Lowood,
however, she is again exposed to injustice and encounters two new ways of
dealing with this, first in the form of Christian forgiveness and meekness,
as embodied in Helen Burns, and secondly submission to social custom, as
embodied in Miss Temple. She takes both on board for a while, but neither
seems to satisfy her. She discovers that she must be true to herself and that
to achieve this she must become independent.

SEARCH FOR IDENTITY

Jane's search for identity takes her to Thornfield where she finds some
happiness, but where she is still restless until the master of the house
appears. After she follows her deepest desires and accepts Rochester's
proposal she becomes acutely sensitive to signs of ill-fortune and is all too
aware of the bad omens that surround their future marriage, but is still
unprepared to deal with the consequences of her actions when the final
calamity falls. When she discovers that Rochester is already married, albeit
to a madwoman, she acts entirely according to convention, as learnt at
Lowood, by fleeing Thornfield in order to regain some self-control. She
does not succumb to passion because her education has shown her that
passion is not a fit motive for action. If she lived with Rochester she would
be a social outcast and lose her partial and hard-won individualism.

SELF-FULFILMENT

For a while, this seems to have been the right move. After the Rivers family
rescue her, she finds all that she ever wanted, money, status, a family, a
home. Hard work and a sound morality are seen to bring their own reward.
However, as St John Rivers asks her to marry him simply for form's sake
and become a missionary's wife, she rediscovers her true self. She finds that
she cannot completely abandon her passions after all. It is only when she
returns to Rochester, having matured and learnt the necessity of combining
desire with duty, that she can live happily ever after. The novel is therefore
about woman's intellectual and emotional needs, the search for identity, and

the way in which passion has to be reconciled with self-control.

We can also see that it is not enough for a woman simply to be respectable or independent.

No matter how rewarding it is for an unmarried woman to make a success of her life through quiet perseverance and a clear moral stand, it is better if she can share her life with an equal, someone who is a companion who will support her and who is dependent on her, and of course the novel ends with a marriage of equals. Rochester's development is important here in helping Jane complete her own growth.

The events that shape the novel therefore test Jane and give the reader the opportunity to explore her deepest motivations and feelings. The plot, characters and language all form an exploration of the theme, but, as we have just seen, to a large extent in this instance, the theme actually dictates the form.

SOCIAL CLASS

Another, less obvious, theme tackles the much broader problem of social class. Though on one level the novel is a love story which covers the experiences of one woman, a representative of her sex, it also deals with the difficulties faced by a particular class of women in Victorian society: young middle-class women – especially governesses – who were poor. Interestingly, it does not really provide these women with a radical solution to their problems.

Though Jane makes a success of her own life, through sheer force of will coupled with a lucky inheritance, she does not offer a way out for those middle-class women who remained poor, or for those who wanted to break the bounds of social convention. She does not save Helen Burns, for instance, whose tendency to self-sacrifice leads to her eventual death, or Eliza Reed who ends up, unsatisfactorily as far as Jane is concerned, in a convent. Most of the other women from her class – including Miss Temple, Miss Oliver and Georgiana Reed – marry according to the prevailing custom of the day by making slightly compromising matches, and we do not even know what happens to others – Miss Ingram, for instance, vanishes without trace.

THE MARRIAGE MARKET

As well as being a governess, Jane (like Charlotte Brontë) was the daughter of a clergyman. Clergymen have always and still do hold a peculiarly ambivalent position in English society, being well educated, having high aspirations, and often the younger sons of 'good families', but *poor*. As a consequence the daughters of clergymen, while frequently mixing with the upper classes would not have been countenanced as potential spouses, either by the upper classes or often even by the middle classes, as they brought no dowry with them. This is why – on a more mundane level – one of the themes of the novel is therefore the 'marriage market'. In this respect the book ends happily because the 'good' win out and find husbands: Jane does, and so do Diana and Mary, Miss Temple and Miss Oliver.

However, in order for this to happen, the would-be brides must have money. This is why Mr Rochester was quite prepared to marry a foreigner whom he hardly knew – he was offered a large sum of money to do so – why it is so seemingly remarkable that Mr Rochester first proposes to Jane and rejects Miss Ingram, and, **ironically**, only legitimately proposes to Jane after their discussion of her inheritance; why after Jane inherits, she is deemed by St John to be a fitting spouse; and why Diana and Mary can marry once Jane has handed over part of her fortune. Jane's fortune, incidentally, would roughly equal a million pounds in today's money.

QUEST FOR LOVE

A further, obvious, theme is Jane's quest for love. Before the novel has even begun Jane has lost the love of her natural parents, as well as that of her uncle, through their respective deaths. Belatedly, she finds a degree of maternal love in Bessie, but quickly loses it again as she is taken off to school at Lowood. She has never experienced any kind of affection from her cousins, but seems to find a sisterly love in Helen Burns, who then dies. Again, she finds a motherly love in Miss Temple, but she loses this when her mentor leaves. Jane therefore decides to move on and once more seems to find a kind of motherly love in Mrs Fairfax, and herself becomes a mother-figure for little Adèle. Mr Rochester, in the meantime, seems to become a dangerous father-figure who then betrays her. She therefore flees Thornfield and finally discovers a lasting sisterly love with Diana and Mary. She at first finds a brotherly love in St John, but soon loses this when he proposes to her. Eventually, of course, Jane finds a passionate and companionable love with Rochester, now reduced to her level through his injuries, blindness and loss of property. One message here seems to be that life and love are basically cruel and that happiness can only truly be achieved at a price. However, Brontë also seems to attack the convention of brotherly and sisterly love as the basis for marriage here, in favour of the new ideal of companionship.

RELIGIOUS FAITH

The novel also, at its core, deals with religious faith – hence the uproar amongst Evangelicals when it was published. It addresses the meaning of religion and its relevance to the individual's behaviour. Jane sees the best and the worst of religious practice at Lowood, encounters a man who wants to reform morality for his own convenience at Thornfield and is finally subject to the juggernaut of religious self-sacrifice at Moor House. Every character who professes some kind of religious faith is placed and subject to some form of ironic commentary. It becomes clear that convention based on social propriety can all too easily be confused with customary behaviour based on religious doctrine. And the novel asks if morality can simply be remade as a social convention, or whether it is something more.

NARRATIVE TECHNIQUE

STRUCTURE

The novel is very tightly constructed and the form has been dictated by its major theme. There is a certain amount of coincidence at work, but only to the extent that coincidences also happen in real life. Brontë wanted to write about what is 'true', in other words what is deeply felt, genuine and sincere, as much as what is observed or 'real' and we can see this in the composition of the novel as much as in its content.

This novel's structure is deceptively organic and free-flowing, and lacks a moral framework which marks a radical departure from the novel

STRUCTURE continued

dominant in Brontë's day. In effect it is given structural unity by Jane, who carries the theme while she searches for a way to build her own identity and resolve the tensions within her character. Because of this and her movements to and from Thornfield, the book falls roughly into five phases, which do not quite correspond with the three volumes of the original edition.

At the end of each phase Jane moves on to a new stage in her development: at Gateshead she is still a child; when she leaves for Lowood she moves into girlhood; she is an adolescent at Thornfield; reaches maturity at Marsh End; and becomes fulfilled with her marriage to Rochester at Ferndean. This structure is suggestive of growth and supports the theme by showing the reader how Jane develops. The structure of the novel is therefore effectively that of a *Bildungsroman,* or 'novel of development', in which the protagonist's growth is traced through childhood, into adulthood and maturity.

There is also some repetition in the novel, however, especially in Jane's flight from Edward Rochester and her flight from St John Rivers. In the thematic structure of the novel, the Jane–Rivers relationship develops in direct contrast to the Jane–Rochester relationship. This enables us to see exactly what is at stake for Jane, who must resolve the tension between passion and self-control in order to live a happy and fulfilled life. On both occasions she struggles to maintain her identity and the two characters effectively symbolise different aspects of her-*self.* The parallels are made clear when she says 'I was almost as hard beset by him [St John] as I had been once before, in a different way, by another.'

NARRATIVE AND POINT OF VIEW

The narrative focuses entirely on Jane, events only appear in the book because they have an impact on her growth into an independent, moral and strong-minded woman and we are only interested in other characters' experiences because Jane can learn from them. Every character and incident therefore has some bearing on her development and, in this way, the theme of the novel is brought alive; every detail is made to count. We are never surprised by a new development of Jane's character: each phase, each element of character development is given a sound basis earlier on in the novel. Plot and character are **foreshadowed**

Because the novel is a fictional autobiography and therefore consists of a first-person narrative we largely see events and characters from the narrator's point of view and this gives the story a high degree of authenticity. This also creates a very close bond between the narrator and the reader and draws the latter into a closer involvement with the story. These petitions to the reader always come at moments of heightened intensity or action, for example when Rochester asks Jane to forgive him after their first wedding-day, 'Reader, I forgave him', when Jane runs away from Rochester afterwards, 'Gentle reader, may you never feel what I felt!', and as we come to the close of the novel, 'Reader, I married him'.

As we have seen in respect of the structure of the novel, it falls roughly into five parts. This works because the novel is set in five different locales: Gateshead, Lowood, Thornfield, Moor House and Ferndean Manor. Each time Jane moves from one locale to another the narrative breaks to set the scene and stress that this setting will form a new stage in Jane's life. It is as if we were moving from one act to another in a five-act drama – an analogy the narrator uses herself in Vol. I, Chapter 11. There are also two scenes in which Jane travels back to a previous locale: from Thornfield to Gateshead, to visit her aunt, and from Moor House to Thornfield, when she searches for Rochester.

Each setting is dominated by a different tone. At Gateshead, for instance, the tone is passionate, superstitious and wild. This reflects the fact that the narrative is focused on a child at this point and shows us the more irrational elements in Jane's character. The tone at Lowood is cold, hard and constrained and reflects the limitations placed on young women by religious thought and social convention. At Thornfield the setting is personal and symbolic, for instance the house itself is identified with Rochester, and the narrative veers between the pacy and the restrained. We feel Jane's pulse quickening as she begins to fall in love with her master, but we are also given a sense of the way in which she is torn between passion and self-control. At Moor House the tone again becomes more stifling and oppressive as Jane slips back into a more conventional way of behaving, and begins to feel the limitations and killing pressure of St John's urge to self-sacrifice. However, when we finally reach Ferndean we move at last from fear and anticipation to delight. The novel therefore oscillates between the irrational – Gateshead and Thornfield – and the rational – Lowood and

Moor House – reflecting the divisions within Jane herself, until resolution is achieved at Ferndean.

LANGUAGE AND STYLE

Brontë wrote very carefully, drafting out every passage before writing it up and she spent a considerable amount of time on small details such as the choice of names. 'Eyre', for instance, came from the Eyre family whose historic house had a room in it which had housed a madwoman, but Brontë used the name because it carried with it the sense of being as free as air, a faint reference to the sprite Ariel and the suggestion of an eagle's eyrie. Where the name 'Reed' suggests a certain pliability, 'Rivers' suggests the pull of strong currents and the influence of forces beyond the individual's control. 'Temple' suggests a place of worship, safety and goodness. 'Jane' hints at 'plain Jane'.

Brontë's language is deceptively simple. Because of her upbringing and early reading, it often has a faintly archaic, eighteenth-century feel to it and tends to be a blend of literary English and Yorkshire dialect. For example, 'e'en took the poor thing' in Vol. I, Chapter 15. This has presented editors with considerable difficulty when correcting her text for publication. For instance, in Vol. III, Chapter 9 Diana says to Jane: 'Tell me what business St John and you have on hands.' This is often changed to 'on hand', but may actually be a local colloquialism.

The descriptive passages of the novel draw us into the action, and though their style is often quite journalistic – 'It was the fifteenth of January, about nine o'clock in the morning: Bessie was gone down to breakfast; my cousins had not yet been summoned to their mama' (Vol. I, Chapter 4) – they are highly suggestive. 'Terrible moment: full of struggle, blackness, burning! Not a human being that ever lived could wish to be loved better than I was loved; and him who thus loved me I absolutely worshipped: and I must renounce love and idol.' (Vol. III, Chapter 1).

The dialogue is especially important because it reflects the education, station and attitude of the characters; with respect to Adèle it is also indicative of her nationality and training. The extensive use of French in the novel adds veracity to Adèle's exchanges with Jane and makes Jane's own accomplishments more tangible. The dialogue also allows us an insight into the minds of the characters, brings them alive and is generally much more convincing than anything written by Brontë's predecessors.

The conversations between Jane and Rochester, for example, feel entirely natural and give us a real sense of their love for each other. Jane and Rochester express themselves very directly, and everything from their banter to their most impassioned exchanges is suggestive of deeply felt and genuine affection. It is also interesting to see how Jane automatically corrects Hannah's English when she first talks to the servant as her superior in Vol. III, Chapter 3:

> 'I am no beggar; any more than yourself or your young ladies.'
>
> After a pause, she said, 'I dunnut understand that: you've like no house, nor no brass, I guess?'
>
> 'The want of house or brass (by which I suppose you mean money) does not make a beggar in your sense of the word.'

This suggests that Jane is acutely sensitive of her social position at this point, and hints at the snobbery of her childhood when she could not 'purchase liberty at the price of caste'.

Brontë's language is at its most powerful when she is describing a mind in torment. The heart of the novel therefore lies in Jane's descriptions of what is going on in her own mind. Her feelings, especially 'conscience' and 'passion', are often given their own voice and they frequently act out a kind of drama or inner morality play within Jane, in which they fight over the right to determine her actions. Vol. III, Chapter 1, in which Jane determines to leave Rochester, provides us with an excellent example of this. These moments of **personification** make us aware of Jane's deepest feelings and help us to understand why she acts as she does.

IMAGERY AND SYMBOLISM

Imagery and symbolism help unite the novel and are as important to the narrative as the action and plot. The novel is full of uncanny, faintly **gothic**, references to local folklore, fairytales, ghosts, and sprites. Jane is driven back to Rochester when she mysteriously hears his voice calling to her when St John Rivers presses her to marry him. But, as noted in Language and Style, the core of the novel actually lies in Jane's descriptions of what goes on in her mind and it is in these descriptions that we find Brontë's most striking use of imagery.

Brontë gets her imagery from literature, especially from Shakespeare and the **Romantics**, the Bible, and, for the large supernatural element in the novel, from her own upbringing. Some images are quite commonplace, but nonetheless when repeated help form clear links between the various characters. Rochester often likens Jane to an eager little bird, for example, meaning she is physically small and mentally agile, but Jane also likens herself to the 'stray and stranger birds' that Rochester throws his crumbs to. After Jane has run away from Rochester, her heart becomes 'impotent as a bird' which, 'with both wings broken … .still quivered its shattered pinions in vain attempts to seek him'. And when the Rivers offer her a home, St John likens her to 'a half-frozen bird, which some wintry wind might have driven through their casement'. When she returns to Rochester she finds that he is like a 'fettered wild beast or bird,' and that, as they enter the final stage of their relationship in which he has to depend on her, he has become 'a royal eagle, chained to a perch' which is 'forced to entreat a sparrow to become its purveyor'.

Another imaginative link, which draws more directly on Brontë's knowledge of folklore, is formed between Jane and Bertha. When Jane sees herself in the mirror of the red-room she sees herself as a ghost, and she is referred to as a sprite and a witch by Rochester. These are quite playful references to the supernatural, but they take on a new import when she herself describes Bertha as a vampire. This feeds into the gothic tone of the Thornfield section of the text and shows us how Jane might herself fall victim to her passions to become another Bertha.

It is interesting to see how Thornfield Hall is often symbolically identified with its master, in appearance, and when it is destroyed. One of the most powerful images in the novel is that of the shattered chestnut tree that stands in its grounds. This tree initially stands as an omen. As a symbol of life it is quite fitting that Rochester proposes to Jane under its boughs. However, split in two by a violent storm that very night it suddenly forewarns us of the disaster to come, of the failed wedding-day and Mr Rochester's injury, and as such fills Jane's thoughts with foreboding before their wedding. It finally reappears at the end of the novel when Rochester proposes for the second time: 'I am no better than the old lightning-struck chestnut-tree in Thornfield orchard.' In other words the tree, initially a simple object in the novel, is transformed by events into a complex image and powerful symbol of Jane and Rochester's relationship.

A key feature of the novel is the symbolic use of literature. We learn a lot about the characters and their situation from what they read. The novel opens on a depressing November afternoon which reflects the depression of Jane Eyre herself who is trying to escape by reading Bewick's *British Birds*. This book is full of images of shipwrecks, storms, Arctic wastes, high mountain reaches, death and disaster and it seems to reflect Jane's own feelings about life at Gateshead. She also reads *Gulliver's Travels* as a kind of escape and the *Arabian Nights* where she learns about magic. Helen Burns, on the other hand, prefers *Rasselas*, a very dry tome about the placid endurance of life and reality. Whereas Jane prefers to read texts that feed into her passions, Helen hopes to learn about the real world and the necessity of self-control.

Part four

Textual analysis

TEXT 1   THE RED-ROOM (VOL. I, CHAPTER 2)

The red-room was a spare chamber, very seldom slept in; I might say never, indeed;
unless when a chance influx of visitors at Gateshead Hall rendered it necessary to
turn to account all the accommodation it contained: yet it was one of the largest and
stateliest chambers in the mansion. A bed supported on massive pillars of mahogany,
hung with curtains of deep-red damask, stood out like a tabernacle in the centre; the
two large windows, with their blinds always drawn down, were half shrouded in
festoons and falls of similar drapery; the carpet was red; the table at the foot of the
bed was covered with a crimson cloth; the walls were a soft fawn colour, with a blush
of pink in it; the wardrobe, the toilet-table, the chairs were of a darkly polished old
mahogany. Out of these deep surrounding shades rose high, and glared white, the
piled-up mattresses and pillows of the bed, spread with a snowy Marseilles
counterpane. Scarcely less prominent was an ample, cushioned easy-chair near the
head of the bed, also white, with a footstool before it; and looking, as I thought, like a
pale throne.

This room was chill, because it seldom had a fire; it was silent, because remote from
the nursery and kitchens; solemn, because it was known to be so seldom entered. The
house-maid alone came here on Saturdays, to wipe from the mirrors and the furniture
a week's quiet dust: and Mrs Reed herself, at far intervals, visited it to review the
contents of a certain secret drawer in the wardrobe, where were stored divers
parchments, her jewel-casket, and a miniature of her deceased husband; and in those
last words lies the secret of the red-room: the spell which kept it so lonely in spite of
its grandeur.

Mr Reed had been dead nine years: it was in this chamber he breathed his last; here
he lay in state; hence his coffin was borne by the undertaker's men; and, since that
day, a sense of dreary consecration had guarded it from frequent intrusion.

My seat, to which Bessie and the bitter Miss Abbot had left me riveted, was a low
ottoman near the marble chimney-piece; the bed rose before me; to my right hand
there was the high, dark wardrobe, with subdued, broken reflections varying the gloss
of its panels; to my left were the muffled windows; a great looking-glass between
them repeated the vacant majesty of the bed and room. I was not quite sure whether
they had locked the door; and, when I dared move, I got up, and went to see. Alas!

Yes: no jail was ever more secure. Returning, I had to cross before the looking-glass; my fascinated glance involuntarily explored the depth it revealed. All looked colder and darker in that visionary hollow than in reality: and the strange little figure there gazing at me, with a white face and arms specking the gloom, and glittering eyes of fear moving where all else was still, had the effect of a real spirit: I thought it like one of the tiny phantoms, half fairy, half imp, Bessie's evening stories represented as coming out of lone, ferny dells in moors, and appearing before the eyes of belated travellers. I returned to my stool.

Superstition was with me at that moment; but it was not yet her hour for complete victory: my blood was still warm; the mood of the revolted slave was still bracing me with its bitter vigour; I had to stem a rapid rush of retrospective thought before I quailed to the dismal present.

This passage comes from early on in *Jane Eyre*. While reading, Jane is disturbed by her cousin John Reed who picks on and throws her book at her. When she retaliates, his sisters call her aunt, Mrs Reed, who locks her in the red-room as punishment. Shortly after this passage ends, Jane loses some of her rebellious fire, becomes frightened and screams. Her aunt leaves her in the room for a further hour, by which time Jane's nerves have collapsed. The servants' apothecary is called in and, after talking with Jane, suggests that she be sent away to boarding school. Jane is an orphan and is being cared for by the Reeds because the late Mr Reed took her in and made Mrs Reed promise him that Jane would continue to live with the family after his death. Mr Reed was Jane's mother's brother.

The Gateshead section of the novel is dominated by a sense of passion, sensuality and superstition, reflecting both Jane's age – she is just ten at this point – and the more irrational side of her character. The self-indulgent Mrs Reed dominates the house, her children are spoilt brats and Jane learns to become as headstrong as the rest of them. In the red-room she begins to discover that there is a down-side to letting her emotions get the better of her, but at this point she is still enjoying their pleasant after-glow of rebellion. Her natural unease at being in her dead uncle's room is, however, gradually being intensified by her superstition and overexcited state of mind.

The tone is initially heavy, as lugubrious as the stately furniture itself while the silence and abandonment of the room is suggested by words like 'subdued', 'muffled', 'vacant'; even the dust is 'quiet'. We see the room from Jane's nervous point of view and she sees the objects within it quite unnaturally. The bed is not simply a bed but becomes a 'tabernacle', the chair beside it becomes 'a pale throne', she herself becomes 'a real spirit', a 'tiny phantom, half fairy, half imp'. Each object metamorphoses into something that is alien and frightening and though the scene is described quite tersely, journalistically, it is also highly suggestive.

The way of seeing described in this passage stays with Jane throughout the novel. Whenever she is unable to explain an experience or other phenomenon she looks for a supernatural or unnatural origin for the marvel. As she matures and learns about it in more detail, she begins to assign the emotion, experience or object a rational explanation. Shortly after this passage ends, for instance, she says that she wondered as a child why she merited such bad treatment from the Reeds; as an adult she is able to reflect on this and explain that it was because she was so unlike them. We are therefore drawn into sympathy for Jane as she sits alone and frightened in a haunted room, but we also gain a more mature understanding of the way in which she has brought much of her ill-treatment upon herself. The point at which she looks into the mirror crystallises one such moment of balanced perception.

The mirror in which she sees herself as a phantom, the punishment of sitting on a chair in a locked and abandoned room for a fit of passion also forms a link between Jane and Mrs Rochester, who is also described as a kind of phantom. The redness of the room itself is symbolic of passion and unreason, and of course it houses secrets – the symbols of Mrs Reed's property and wealth – just like the attic at Thornfield Hall. This prefigures the link that is established between Jane and Bertha when Jane wanders, daydreaming on the third storey at Thornfield – 'if there were a ghost at Thornfield, this would be its haunt' – and suggests that if she had not learnt to control her irrational instincts and had stayed with Edward Rochester, then she would have also have become, if not actually a madwoman, then as powerless and lacking in the ability to control her own life as a madwoman.

TEXT 2   ROCHESTER'S PROPOSAL (VOL. II, CHAPTER 8)

'Come – we'll talk over the voyage and the parting quietly, half an hour or so, while the stars enter into their shining life up in heaven yonder: here is the chestnut tree; here is the bench at its old roots. Come, we will sit there in peace to-night, though we should never more be destined to sit there together.' He seated me and himself.
'It is a long way to Ireland, Janet, and I am sorry to send my little friend on such weary travels: but if I can't do better, how is it to be helped? Are you anything akin to me, do you think, Jane?'
I could risk no sort of answer by this time: my heart was full.
'Because,' he said, 'I sometimes have a queer feeling with regard to you – especially when you are near me, as now: it is as if I had a string somewhere under my left ribs, tightly and inextricably knotted to a similar string situated in the corresponding quarter of your little frame. And if that boisterous channel, and two hundred miles or so of land come broad between us, I am afraid that cord of communion will be snapt; and then I've a nervous notion I should take to bleeding inwardly. As for you, – you'd forget me.'
'That I *never* should, sir: you know –' impossible to proceed.
'Jane, do you hear that nightingale singing in the wood? Listen!'
In listening, I sobbed convulsively; for I could repress what I endured no longer; I was obliged to yield, and I was shaken from head to foot with acute distress. When I did speak, it was only to express an impetuous wish that I had never been born, or never come to Thornfield.
'Because you are sorry to leave it?'
The vehemence of emotion, stirred by grief and love within me, was claiming mastery, and struggling for full sway; and asserting a right to predominate: to overcome, to live, rise, and reign at last; yes, – and to speak.
'I grieve to leave Thornfield: I love Thornfield: – I love it, because I have lived in it a full and delightful life, – momentarily at least. I have not been trampled upon. I have not been petrified. I have not been buried with inferior minds, and excluded from every glimpse of communion with what is bright and energetic, and high. I have talked, face to face, with what I reverence; with what I delight in, – with an original, a vigorous, an expanded mind. I have known you, Mr Rochester; and it strikes me with terror and anguish to feel I absolutely must be torn from you for ever. I see the necessity of departure; and it is like looking on the necessity of death.'
'Where do you see the necessity?' he asked, suddenly.
'Where? You, sir, have placed it before me.'

'In what shape?'

'In the shape of Miss Ingram; a noble and beautiful woman, – your bride.'

'My bride! What bride? I have no bride!'

'But you will have.'

'Yes; – I will! I will!' He set his teeth.

'Then I must go: – you have said it yourself.'

'No: you must stay! I swear it – and the oath shall be kept.'

'I tell you I must go!' I retorted, roused to something like passion. 'Do you think I can stay to become nothing to you? Do you think I am an automaton? – a machine without feelings? and can bear to have my morsel of bread snatched from my lips, and my drop of living water dashed from my cup? Do you think, because I am poor, obscure, plain, and little, I am soulless and heartless? – You think wrong! – I have as much soul as you, – and full as much heart! And if God had gifted me with some beauty, and much wealth, I should have made it as hard for you to leave me, as it is now for me to leave you. I am not talking to you now through the medium of custom, conventionalities, nor even of mortal flesh: – it is my spirit that addresses your spirit; just as if both had passed through the grave, and we stood at God's feet, equal – as we are!'

'As we are! Repeated Mr Rochester – 'so,' he added, enclosing me in his arms, gathering me to his breast, pressing his lips on my lips: 'so, Jane!'

'Yes, so, sir,' I rejoined: 'and yet not so; for you are a married man – or as good as a married man, and wed to one inferior to you – to one with whom you have no sympathy – whom I do not believe you truly love; for I have seen and heard you sneer at her. I would scorn such a union: therefore I am better than you – let me go!'

'Where, Jane? To Ireland?'

'Yes – to Ireland. I have spoken my mind, and can go anywhere now.'

'Jane, be still; don't struggle so, like a wild, frantic bird that is rending its own plumage in its desperation.'

'I am no bird; and no net ensnares me: I am a free human being with an independent will; which I now exert to leave you.'

Another effort set me at liberty, and I stood erect before him.

'And your will shall decide your destiny,' he said: 'I offer you my hand, my heart, and a share of all my possessions.'

This passage comes almost midway through *Jane Eyre*. By this point Jane has left Gateshead and has since spent eight years at Lowood school, as pupil and then teacher, where she has learnt about self-sacrifice from her friend Helen Burns and self-control from her teacher Miss Temple. After advertising for a place as a governess she accepted a position at Thornfield Hall.

Jane and the master of Thornfield, Mr Edward Fairfax Rochester, have gradually become friends and, while taking some time off to visit her dying aunt, Jane has discovered that she has fallen in love with him. However, as far as she is concerned, Mr Rochester is too far above her in station for anything to come of this, and she expects him to marry a local heiress, Miss Blanche Ingram – partly because of rumours he has himself circulated to test Jane's feelings.

It is sunset on Midsummer's eve and the garden is full of sweet scents and song, but soon after Jane accepts Rochester's proposal the chestnut tree is split in two by a violent storm. The wedding is interrupted and called off when it is suddenly revealed that Mr Rochester is already married. His wife is a madwoman kept under lock-and-key, but Jane cannot countenance his attempted bigamy and flees.

As Jane gradually moves, Eve-like, from innocence to understanding we are provided with a lyrical example of the naturalistic dialogue that regularly takes place between the two lovers. Their conversations bring the characters alive and through them Brontë makes a complete break with the novels of her time. Where other authors avoided this kind of complex exchange, by glossing over the characters' speeches or using paraphrase, and some produced only a stilted and clumsy impression of speech, Brontë manages to move rapidly and confidently between confusion, explanation, and exclamation in such a way as to allow us to understand Jane's turmoil and Rochester's own inner conflict.

Jane is quite powerless, given her social position, but speaks as an individual who demands to be treated with respect and fights to maintain her identity – 'I am no bird;... I am a free human being with an independent will' – and so talks on behalf of her sex. She does not want to be exiled, but fights for her self-respect by demanding that she be permitted to leave rather than watch Rochester enter a conventional marriage based on property. In the process she rehearses her history to date: 'I have not been trampled on. I have not been petrified. I have not been buried with inferior minds'. She is trying to reconcile passion with duty, 'and it is like looking on the necessity of death'.

Rochester, half talking to Jane, half thinking out loud – 'if I can't do better, how is it to be helped?' – tests her love and is working up to asking her for her hand. The reason for his hesitation becomes clear on their wedding-day, and is unwittingly **foreshadowed** by Jane – 'you are a married man … and wed to one inferior to you' – while she still thinks he intends to marry Miss Ingram. **Ironically**, Miss Ingram does in fact look like and behave as his wife did before she went mad.

In loving Jane, Rochester hopes to find Bertha's antithesis – 'the antipodes of the Creole'. Though Jane has begun to mature and combine passion with self-control, however, Rochester has yet to learn from his experiences or face the consequences of his actions. As he pours out his love against the nightingale's song, he still needs to realise that Jane will only love him in return if he treats her with respect. Though his love is quite genuine, his proposal is essentially built on a secret and is therefore enslaving, dishonourable and shallow: the Midsummer's fairytale is about to go wrong.

At this point Jane and Rochester are doomed, as is soon suggested in the storm that breaks out over their heads. The chestnut tree under which Jane and Rochester sit is a symbol of life, but quickly becomes an omen of ill-fortune and they are chased out of the paradisiacal garden as Rochester asks God to sanction their marriage. The Thornfield section of the novel is often simultaneously personal and symbolic in this way. Rochester gives Thornfield Hall life and a sense of purpose when he is there, but it is also symbolically identified with him. When Jane first tours the building there are vague foreshadowings of what she will find out about it and its master. By the end of the novel, when he has finally learnt his lesson, Rochester likens his own maimed body to the shriven tree's black form.

TEXT 3   ST JOHN'S PROPOSAL (VOL. III, CHAPTER 9)

I stood motionless under my hierophant's touch. My refusals were forgotten – my fears overcome – my wrestlings paralysed. The Impossible – *i.e.* my marriage with St John – was fast becoming the Possible. All was changing utterly, with a sudden sweep. Religion called – Angels beckoned – God commanded – life rolled together like a scroll – death's gates opening, shewed eternity beyond: it seemed, that for safety and bliss there, all here might be sacrificed in a second. The dim room was full of visions.

'Could you decide now?' asked the missionary. The inquiry was put in gentle tones: he drew me to him as gently. Oh, that gentleness! how far more potent is it than force! I could resist St John's wrath: I grew pliant as a reed under his kindness. Yet I knew all the time, if I yielded now, I should not the less be made to repent, some day, of my former rebellion. His nature was not changed by one hour of solemn prayer: it was only elevated.

'I could decide if I were but certain,' I answered: 'were I but convinced that it is God's will I should marry you, I could vow to marry you here and now – come afterwards what would!'

'My prayers are heard!' ejaculated St John. He pressed his hand firmer on my head, as if he claimed me: he surrounded me with his arm, *almost* as if he loved me (I say *almost* – I knew the difference – for I had felt what it was to be loved; but, like him, I had now put love out of the question, and thought only of duty): I contended with my inward dimness of vision, before which clouds yet rolled. I sincerely, deeply, fervently longed to do what was right; and only that. 'Shew me, shew me the path!' I entreated of Heaven. I was excited more than I had ever been; and whether what followed was the effect of excitement, the reader will judge.

All the house was still; for I believe all, except St John and myself, were now retired to rest. The one candle was dying out: the room was full of moonlight. My heart beat fast and thick: I heard its throb. Suddenly it stood still to an inexpressible feeling that thrilled it through, and passed at once to my head and extremities. The feeling was not like an electric shock; but it was quite as sharp, as strange, as startling: it acted on my senses as if their utmost activity hitherto had been but torpor; from which they were now summoned, and forced to wake. They rose expectant: eye and ear waited, while the flesh quivered on my bones.

'What have you heard? What do you see?' asked St John. I saw nothing: but I heard a voice somewhere cry –

'Jane! Jane! Jane!' nothing more.

'Oh God! What is it?' I gasped.

I might have said, 'Where is it?' for it did not seem in the room – nor in the house – nor in the garden: it did not come out of the air – nor from under the earth – nor from overhead. I had heard it – where, or whence, for ever impossible to know! And it was the voice of a human being – a known, loved, well-remembered voice – that of Edward Fairfax Rochester; and it spoke in pain and woe wildly, eerily, urgently.

'I am coming!' I cried. 'Wait for me! Oh, I will come!'

The passage comes from the latter half of *Jane Eyre*. After the abortive marriage ceremony at Thornfield, Jane feels that she must leave the hall. Having used all her money and losing her possessions in her escape, she wanders destitute for several days, forced to beg for help. She is turned away by everyone, until, starving and cold, St John Rivers takes her in. She and his two sisters, Mary and Diana, become friends and he offers her the post of local schoolmistress. She does not like the work but accepts the position.

During this period in her life she lives by the name Jane Elliott, but when Rivers discovers her true identity he is able to tell her that she has inherited a fortune. He knows this because they are in fact related and Jane promptly shares out the money equally between herself and the others. After this Mary and Diana treat her like a sister and St John begins to teach her Hindustani. Eventually he proposes.

St John wants her to go with him to India as a missionary's wife. She says she will go as his sister, but he will only take her if she will marry him. In this passage he presses her on the subject again, but, after hearing the mysterious voice, she determines to find out what has become of Rochester. She goes back to Thornfield and discovers that it has been destroyed by fire, its master maimed in the attempt to save his wife who has fallen to her death. She seeks out Rochester and finally they marry.

St John is as hard and 'cold as an iceberg', he is 'marble' – in opposition to Mr Brocklehurst who is 'a black pillar' – but in this passage he becomes gentle in an attempt to draw Jane into his plans. The setting is eerie and faintly unnatural: the room in which Jane and St John stand is dark, except for a guttering candle and the moonlight; outside all is black and silent except for the soughing March wind. It is night-time and everyone else has retired to bed. The language is journalistic and the tone of the piece is tense, thrilling, but quite unlike that of the garden scene in which Rochester proposed.

St John is utterly unable to bend himself to the yoke of mutual love and tenderness, and as such, is the opposite of Mr Rochester who helps Jane to the full enjoyment of life – as she herself recognises in parenthesis. There is no sympathy between them, St John simply tries to dominate Jane – 'He pressed his hand firmer on my head, as if he claimed me' – and, as we can see from the self-conscious stress on *'almost'*, only ever gives the appearance of love. He may seem to be a high-minded clergyman, but he is actually a thug who is determined that others will submit to his will and sacrifice themselves to his cause – 'My prayers are heard!' he cries as she says she *might* marry him.

Jane has already seen through the gloss of right-minded missionary to the ambitious man within – 'I should not the less be made to repent, some day, of my former rebellion' – but she still finds it hard to withstand his assaults on her own hard-won identity. This is because she wants to do what is morally right. Through St John and Jane's relationship Brontë exposes the Victorian myth of self-denying asceticism which, juxtaposed against a real and deeply felt morality that has nothing to do with social convention, is shown to equate with the heartless sacrifice of others.

Where Rochester tempted Jane to throw away social convention and duty, so St John tempts her to throw away her passion, to renounce her nature entirely. And because fate has brought them together she finds it hard to see clearly whether or not she should marry him – 'I contended with my inward dimness of vision, before which clouds yet rolled'. However, Rochester's love is transcendent. And, as Jane cries to Heaven for help, so she receives her aid and escapes his death-willing vision of faith. Where Rochester called out to God to sanction the bigamous marriage, St John calls on God to support his own shallow and essentially meaningless proposal. Where Providence previously spoke through the destruction of the chestnut tree, this time Jane hears Rochester's voice.

PART FIVE

BACKGROUND

CHARLOTTE BRONTË AND HER WORKS

Charlotte Brontë (1816–55) was the third of five daughters born to Patrick Brontë and Maria Branwell. Born in Northern Ireland Patrick Brontë had taken a scholarship in England to become a Church of England clergyman and, after working as a curate, finally became Rector of Haworth on the Yorkshire Moors in 1820. Her mother and Aunt Elizabeth came from a prominent Cornish, Methodist family. Charlotte's younger sisters, Anne and Emily Brontë, also became authors. Their mother died in 1821 and after this they and their brother Branwell were looked after by their mother's sister Elizabeth Branwell.

Charlotte was initially educated at home, then sent to a boarding school for clergymen's daughters at Cowan Bridge with her two elder sisters Maria and Elizabeth, and Emily. Maria and Elizabeth died of tuberculosis there in 1825. Because their illness had been made worse by lack of food and the unhealthy conditions at the school Charlotte and Emily were removed. Charlotte then stayed at home for several years. During this time she read widely with her family and invented an imaginary world with Branwell called Angria. Charlotte, Emily, Anne and Branwell wrote a large amount of poetry, drama and prose over this period, 1829–31.

In 1831 Charlotte went to Miss Wooler's school at Roe Head, where she became an assistant teacher in 1835. She disliked the work and, from 1839 to 1841, attempted to make a living as a governess. She and her sisters hoped in the long run to open their own school and, with her aunt's help, she and Emily travelled to Brussels in 1842 in order to study languages. They returned at the end of the year due to her aunt's illness. During this time they had had no enquiries about their school, so Charlotte went back to Brussels on her own in 1843 to work as an English teacher. During this time her letters reveal that she became close to her tutor Monsieur Heger.

Charlotte returned home in 1844 in order to care for her father who, by this point, was nearly blind. Shortly after this she discovered her sister Emily's poetry in 1845. Charlotte had already begun to write her own verse, so she organised the publication in 1846 of *Poems by Currer, Ellis and Acton*

Bell – the assumed names of Charlotte, Emily and Anne. The verse did not sell well and Charlotte's first novel *The Professor* which she began in 1846 was not published until much later, but *Jane Eyre* (1847) was an immediate success.

Branwell and Emily died in 1848, followed by Anne in 1849, but Charlotte continued to write. Charlotte also published *Shirley*, a **condition of England novel** set in Yorkshire during the period of the Luddite riots at the end of the Napoleonic era. This was followed by *Villette* (1853) and *The Professor* (1857) both of which draw on her life in Brussels. She visited London in 1849, 1850, 1851 and 1853 and made her mark on the literary circles of her day. It was during this period of her life that Charlotte met Thackeray, to whom she had dedicated *Jane Eyre*, G.H. Lewes, and Harriet Martineau, and became friends with her future biographer Elizabeth Gaskell. Though some critics said Charlotte was too 'strong-minded' and coarse, she was generally recognised as a powerful and talented writer by her contemporaries.

Charlotte received three proposals during her life, but finally married her father's curate, Arthur Bell Nicholls, in 1854. She died during pregnancy a few months later, in March 1855.

HISTORICAL BACKGROUND

Jane Eyre is an advocate for her sex at a time when women's talents, skills and independence were far from being valued. Charlotte Brontë was well aware of women's subservient position in Victorian society and of the difficulties that were faced by a woman who wanted to make her way in the world. At this point it was not respectable for a middle-class woman to earn her own living: she was expected to make a career out of marriage or at least to confine her public interests to doing unpaid charitable work. If a young middle-class woman had to support herself and wanted to maintain her class position and reputation, she really only had one option: to work as a governess. The governess was therefore in an anomalous social position because she was neither a servant, due to her class, nor a proper young lady.

Brontë was especially sensitive to the difficulties faced by these young women because she herself had worked as a teacher and as a governess, and hoped to make a career out of writing. This lends a special poignancy to

Jane's story as in many respects it was based on Charlotte Brontë's own experience. Brontë also read widely on the subject of woman's position thanks to the large number of articles and books that were being published on this issue in the 1840s. It would not be useful to overemphasise the significance of the author's biography here, Brontë herself said that though Jane Eyre looked like her, they had nothing else in common, but the theme of the novel was deeply felt by Brontë and this should be borne in mind.

LITERARY BACKGROUND

Charlotte Brontë read widely as a child and as a young woman while she lived at home in her father's rectory at Haworth. She, her brother and sisters were encouraged to dip into Aesop, the Bible, Homer, Virgil, Shakespeare, Milton, Thomson, Goldsmith, Pope, Byron, Scott, Southey, Wordsworth, *The Arabian Nights' Entertainments*, Campbell, plus critical and political articles published in periodicals such as *Blackwood's Magazine*, *Fraser's Magazine*, and *The Edinburgh Review*. They also read from illustrated annuals such as *The Gem*, *The Amulet*, and *Friendship's Offering*.

Charlotte Brontë may have lost the strong religious sensibility of her earlier years by the time that she wrote *Jane Eyre*, but her early literary training continued to be influential in all her novels. The sagas, poetry and dramas that the Brontë children wrote provide ample evidence of the influence of this diverse reading and are full of **melodrama** passion, the weird and wonderful, and keenly felt moral themes. This helps explain why *Jane Eyre* seems to be a mixture of **gothic realist** and **Romantic**

Charlotte continued to read widely throughout her lifetime but there do appear to be some interesting gaps in her literary history. For instance, at the time that *Jane Eyre* was being written, Jane Austen was already a well-established author, but it does not appear that Charlotte had read her. The critic G.H. Lewes in fact advised Charlotte to read some of Austen's work in order to improve her own writing. When Charlotte finished *Pride and Prejudice*, however, she wrote to Lewes explaining that Austen was altogether useless to her and was not even, really, a novelist, as she was 'without poetry'. Austen, Brontë argued, was 'only shrewd and observant', she was 'sensible, real (more *real* than *true*) but she cannot be great'. It is difficult to know exactly who Charlotte Brontë read in later life, but we know from the dedication which appears in the second edition that she read Thackeray who, like Trollope, George Eliot and Dickens, shared her dislike of Evangelicalism, while Mrs Gaskell was of course her friend and later her biographer.

PART SIX

CRITICAL HISTORY

RECEPTION AND EARLY CRITICAL REVIEWS

Jane Eyre was well received and a bestseller when it was first published. But there was also widespread censure of the novel on social and moral grounds due to its critical representation of religious sentiment, its easy acceptance of a love which transcends class, and, finally, its author's vivid portrayal of emotion. Elizabeth Rigby, for instance, writing for a conservative periodical, the *Quarterly Review* in 1848, felt that 'the tone of mind and thought which has overthrown authority and violated every code human and divine ... is the same which has also written *Jane Eyre*'.

Thus, in the 1840s, *Jane Eyre* was a revolutionary text. Victorian critics did not like Jane Eyre's strong-minded independence and many thought that the novel was coarse. The novel was blamed for the corruption of contemporary tastes and morality, in both life and art. Most contemporary critics felt that there was something dangerous in the novel's underlying message, while Jane Eyre herself was seen as godless and unrestrained. Others thought that Brontë's personality was reflected in the novel and that that personality was irredeemably coarse, vulgar and alien.

EARLY TWENTIETH-CENTURY VIEWS

Up until the 1970s twentieth-century critics like Lord David Cecil in *Early Victorian Novelists* (Constable, 1934) were quite scathing in their assessment of *Jane Eyre* because of the way in which the novel operates, in part, as a fairytale or as a simple narrative of wish fulfilment. This, in their view, put the novel beyond the bounds of a serious adult readership while, at the same time, they accused it of being a baggy, rather artless blend of undisciplined daydreams. Brontë is supposed to have written incoherently, without form, restraint, observation or analysis. The narrative is said to be held up by unnecessary passages of over-poetic prose. The plot is accused of moving forward thanks to a combination of good luck and coincidence, while the novel itself is assumed to lack composition. However, others, like

Q.D. Leavis in her introduction to the Penguin edition of *Jane Eyre* in 1966, have stood up for the novel and argued that it is in fact very tightly composed, and that its structure is coherent and thoroughly controlled in the interest of the theme. In it, Jane Eyre's world, her thoughts and feelings are not simply observed, but, more importantly, imagined on the deepest level.

MARXIST CRITICISM

During the 1970s new readings of the novel began to emerge, most notably those of Marxists and feminists. Marxist critics, like Raymond Williams in *The English Novel: from Dickens to Lawrence* (Chatto & Windus, 1970) and Terry Eagleton in *Myths of Power: a Marxist study of the Brontës* (Macmillan, 1975), reassessed the context in which Brontë's books were written and read. Williams stresses that the period in which the Brontë sisters were writing was one of unprecedented social change. The tensions of this period, he argues, are reflected both in the representation of desire and in the fear of isolation that we see in *Jane Eyre*. The novel's passion is then communicated through a kind of private conversation between narrator and reader and this, in his view, is what makes it new. Eagleton, in turn, argues that the central problem or key theme in *Jane Eyre* is submission and the point at which this ceases to be a good thing. Charlotte Brontë, in Eagleton's view, sought a balance between the social and moral conventions of her day and self-fulfilment. Due to this, in *Jane Eyre*, Jane negotiates her way between these opposing urges and manages to climb the social ladder, quite properly – thanks to an inheritance and good behaviour – *and* on her own terms.

FEMINIST CRITICISM

Feminists, in their turn, have read *Jane Eyre* as a radical text in which a woman writer has successfully written about the treatment of women in her society. In this way modern critics, like Sandra Gilbert and Susan Gubar in *The Madwoman in the Attic: the woman writer and the nineteenth-century literary imagination* (Yale University Press, 1979), have picked up on the issues that so distressed the book's original, Victorian critics. Most commentators in fact now tend to stress the underlying political purpose of the novel in which Jane acts as an advocate for women. This works because, though the plot is like that of a fairytale, it has been transposed to the real world in which Cinderella's story has quite different and radical implications to those it has when it is safely tucked away in never-never land. Gilbert and Gubar therefore say that Mrs Rigby's assessment of *Jane Eyre*, quoted above, is quite correct, whether or not the author wanted to admit it at the time.

Not all criticism comes in the form of non-fiction prose, of course, and *Jane Eyre* has also been rewritten as a novel. Jean Rhys's *The Wide Sargasso Sea* (1966) tells the story from the first Mrs Rochester's point of view, rather than Jane's, and provides the reader with a very different understanding of the original narrative.

CONTEMPORARY APPROACHES

Psychoanalytical readings and those which focus on myth have suggested many new and interesting readings of the novel, including the idea that Rochester's first wife is Jane's double. Bertha Mason is a madwoman who is kept under lock and key in the attic, is unable to speak, physically and mentally resembles a savage wild animal and is treated as a thing rather than as a human being. She therefore seems to be the opposite of Jane who is a calm English governess, rational, self-controlled, articulate and small. However, as Elizabeth Imlay has noted in *Charlotte Brontë and the Mysteries of Love: myth and allegory in Jane Eyre* (Harvester Wheatsheaf, 1989), both women are represented at different times in very similar ways.

Jane describes Bertha as a ghost or a vampire after the wedding veil is torn. This is a very frightening image, but Mr Rochester similarly thinks of Jane as an imp, spirit and witch. Bertha is mad, and Jane is said to behave like a mad cat; Bertha scratches and bites, and Jane scratches her cousin John Reed; Bertha is tied to a chair and locked in a room, Jane is told to sit in a chair and is locked in the red-room. In other words, when Jane follows her passions and loses her self-control, she behaves and is punished like Bertha. When she is frustrated by her life at Thornfield Jane goes up onto the third floor to daydream, at which point she is physically and mentally close to Bertha. In this way we become aware of the fact that Jane could easily become another madwoman if she followed her basest instincts. Bertha's death, at which point Rochester is also maimed and tamed, therefore symbolises the sacrifice of the most passionate part of Jane's self.

Recently critics like Edward Said in *Orientalism* (Pantheon, 1978) have also highlighted the importance of colonialism and images of imperialism and empire in *Jane Eyre*. For example, Jane is clearly a white middle-class Protestant who believes in healthy good deeds and hard work. When she runs away from Thornfield she therefore says that she will try to turn her hand to anything that is honest. However, she still draws the line at travelling to India where, she fears, she would collapse and die, as St John eventually does. This rational approach to life allows her to have the self-control that Bertha Mason lacks.

Bertha Mason's story is itself a colonial narrative. Rochester marries her purely for her property. In fact, he goes to the Caribbean just to seek his fortune and, like other English adventurers, found unbridled passion and madness as well as a solution to his financial difficulties. Interestingly, until Rochester meets Jane all his sexual partners have been foreign, and this is typical of the period. Foreign women were supposed to be more highly sexed than English women, but, more importantly, the very fact that they were foreign also made them particularly attractive to English men. Foreign shores and people were seen as dangerous, essentially unhealthy, wild, yet alluring in the British novels of the time, and Charlotte Brontë has made full use of this widespread colonial imagery. Bertha is a thing rather than a human being because she is a Creole, not just because she is a madwoman. And, as suggested by Rochester's desperate need to leave the West Indies, only Britain can provide a safe haven for the English.

PART SEVEN

BROADER PERSPECTIVES

FURTHER READING

Some general books on the Brontë sisters provide further useful insights:

Inga-Stina Ewbank, *Their Proper Sphere, A Study of the Brontë Sisters as Early-Victorian Female Novelists*, Edward Arnold, 1996

Places Charlotte and her sisters in their historical context

Robert Bernard Martin, *The Accents of Persuasion; Charlotte Brontë's Novels*, Faber and Faber, 1966

A good traditional account

Elaine Showalter, *A Literature of Their Own*, Princeton University Press, 1977

A useful introduction to women's writing in the nineteenth century

Tony Tanner, 'Passion, Narrative and Identity in *Wuthering Heights* and *Jane Eyre*', in *Contemporary Approaches to Narrative*, ed. Anthony Mortimer, Tübingen, 1984

A valuable survey of some of the key issues

P.Boumelha, *Charlotte Brontë*, Harvester, 1990

An excellent biography, as is Elizabeth Gaskell, *Life of Charlotte Brontë* 1857, Penguin Classics, 1998

History	Charlotte's life	Literature
1811 First Luddite riot, Nottingham		
	1812 Patrick Brontë, an Irish protestant clergyman marries Maria Branwell, a Cornish methodist from Penzance	
1813-17 Luddites executed, York. Movement broken	**1813** Birth of Maria **1813-18** Patrick publishes a collection of poems and two novels	**1813** Jane Austen, *Pride and Prejudice*
1815 Napoleon escapes from Elba, becomes Emperor and is defeated at Waterloo	**1815** Birth of Elizabeth	**1815** Byron, *Completed Works*
	1816 Birth of Charlotte	**1816** Jane Austen, *Emma*
	1817 Birth of Branwell	**1817** Death of Jane Austen
	1818 Birth of Emily **1819** The Brontë family move to Haworth in Yorkshire	**1818** Mary Shelley, *Frankenstein*
1820 Death of George III (end of Regency), and accession of George IV, who attempts to dissolve his marriage to Caroline. Death of Napoleon	**1820** Birth of Anne	
	1821 Mrs Maria Brontë dies of cancer, and her sister, Elizabeth Branwell, comes to care for the children	**1821** Death of poet, John Keats
		1824 Death of poet, Lord Byron
1825 First railway opened between Stockton and Darlington	**1825** Both Maria and Elizabeth die of tuberculosis at Cowan Bridge School	
1829 Catholic emancipation in Britain		
1830 Death of George IV and accession of William IV		

History	Charlotte's life	Literature
1830s Abolitionists of Slave Trade active in America; articles in *Monthly Repository* by W.J. Fox and W.B. Adams influenced by Harriet Taylor		
1831 Cholera epidemic	**1831** Charlotte boards at Roe Head school, Mirfield	
1832 First Reform Act		**1832** Death of Walter Scott and Goethe; Harriet Martineau, *Illustrations of Political Economy*; Anna Jameson, *Characteristics of Women*
1833 Slavery abolished		
1834 Establishment of Union Workhouses; Tolpuddle Martyrs		
	1835-8 Charlotte returns to Roe Head as a teacher, with Emily as a pupil, but after 3 months of homesickness Emily returns to Haworth	
		1836 Charles Dickens, *The Pickwick Papers*
1837 Death of William IV; accession of Queen Victoria		
1838 'People's Charter' published		
1839 Chartist petition rejected by Parliament - riots, Birmingham	**1839** Charlotte, now a governess, visits Norton Conyers, near Rippon, model for Thornfield Hall. Charlotte turns down two proposals of marriage: from her friend Ellen Nussey's clergyman brother, and from an Irish clergyman	
1840 Penny Post established		**1840** Death of novelist, Fanny Burney
	1841 Charlotte becomes governess to a family near Bradford	
1842 Second Chartist petition presented and rejected	**1842** Charlotte and Emily study French in Brussels at Mme Heger's school	
	1843 Charlotte returns to Brussels to teach and falls in love with Monsieur Heger	**1843** Margaret Fuller (American journalist), 'The Great Lawsuit - Man versus Men. Woman versus Women', *The Dial*

History	Charlotte's life	Literature
	1844 Charlotte returns home when her father becomes almost totally blind	
1845 Famine in Ireland due to potato blight		**1845** Margaret Fuller, *Women in the Nineteenth Century*
1846 Repeal of Corn Laws	**1846** *Poems by Currer, Ellis and Acton Bell* are published by the three sisters	**1846** Margaret Fuller visits Britain
	1847 Charlotte's *Jane Eyre* is published under the pseudonym of Currer Bell; Anne's *Agnes Grey* is published under the pseudonym of Acton Bell; Emily's *Wuthering Heights* is published under the pseudonym of Ellis Bell	**1847** William Thackeray, *Vanity Fair* (serialisation)
1848 Final Chartist petition rejected. Revolutions in Paris, Berlin, Vienna, Venice, Rome, Milan, Naples, Prague and Budapest; Marx and Engel, *Communist Manifesto*	**1848** Anne's *The Tenant of Wildfell Hall* is published; Branwell dies of alcoholism; Emily dies of tuberculosis	**1848** Elizabeth Gaskell, *Mary Burton*
1849 Cholera epidemic	**1849** Anne dies of tuberculosis, leaving Charlotte as the only surviving sibling; Charlotte publishes *Shirley*	**1849-54** *Eliza Cook's Journal*
	1849-51 Charlotte visits London and meets writers of her day: Mrs Gaskell, Harriet Martineau, William Thackeray	
1851 The Great Exhibition at the Crystal Palace		**1851** Harriet Taylor, 'Enfranchisement of Women', in *Westminster Review*
		1852 Harriet Beecher Stowe, *Uncle Tom's Cabin*
	1853 Charlotte publishes *Villette,* based on her experiences in Brussels	
1854 Cholera epidemic	**1854** Charlotte marries her father's curate, Arthur Nicholls	
	1855 Charlotte is pregnant, but dies from a combination of ill health and pneumonia, before reaching full term	

Y

Bildungsroman a novel describing the progress of a character from childhood to maturity and focusing on the relationship between character, experience, education and identity

closure the feeling of completeness and finality achieved by the ending of some literary works; especially associated with the classic realist texts of the nineteenth century

condition of England novel a novel of the 1840s and 1850s which tries to tackle the pressing social issues of the day, in particular the plight of the urban poor

denouement final unfolding of the plot

expository from 'exposition', i.e., an explanation or to do with the delivery of information

foreshadow prefigure a later event or turning point

gothic in the eighteenth century used to describe any work of art which appeared fantastic or eerie

irony a form of sarcasm. Saying one thing and meaning another. A norm is established and then subverted

melodramatic like melodrama, aimed to excite through incident and strong but simple feelings, with clearly 'good' or 'bad' characters and always ending happily

metaphysical to do with the immaterial; or philosophy that there is something beyond or independent of the human; the abstract, sometimes the supernatural

pathos suffering feeling; that quality in a work of art that arouses pity and sadness

personification a figurative language in which ideas, feelings or things are treated as if they were human beings

point of view seen from the viewpoint or through they eyes of a particular character

realist a realist author represents the world as it is rather than as it should be, using description rather than invention; observes and documents everyday life in straightforward prose, draws on characters from all levels of society, but often from the lowest classes, represents their speech and manners accurately. Realism became the dominant form of literature in the nineteenth century

Romantics Romanticism covers a range of tendencies in literature, art and culture that emerged at the end of the eighteenth century and dominated the early years of the nineteenth century. Generally, it involved a movement away from the sceptical, rational, formal culture of the eighteenth century and aimed to liberate the creative imagination. The Romantics rejected the limitations of form and precedent and saw themselves as individuals who could express themselves according to their imagination. They explored everything that was felt to be mysterious, remote, unnerving, and assumed the mantle of prophets and legislators; the poet became a special kind of person, set apart from other people because of them. They saw nature as unmodified by humanity, inherently dazzling and elevating; and believed that humanity should learn from nature personified as 'Nature'

AUTHOR OF THIS NOTE

Karen Sayer lectures in the Department of Literary Studies at the Univerity of Luton. She took her first degree at Portsmouth Polytechnic and studied for her D.Phil at the University of Sussex. Her first monograph *Women of the Fields* was published by Manchester University Press in 1995; *A Cottage in the Country* is in preparation.

NOTES

York Notes Advanced (£3.99 each)

Margaret Atwood
The Handmaid's Tale

Jane Austen
Emma

Jane Austen
Pride and Prejudice

William Blake
Songs of Innocence and of Experience

Charlotte Brontë
Jane Eyre

Emily Brontë
Wuthering Heights

Geoffrey Chaucer
The Wife of Bath's Prologue and Tale

Joseph Conrad
Heart of Darkness

Charles Dickens
Great Expectations

F. Scott Fitzgerald
The Great Gatsby

Thomas Hardy
Tess of the d'Urbervilles

Seamus Heaney
Selected Poems

James Joyce
Dubliners

Arthur Miller
Death of a Salesman

William Shakespeare
Antony and Cleopatra

William Shakespeare
Hamlet

William Shakespeare
King Lear

William Shakespeare
The Merchant of Venice

William Shakespeare
Much Ado About Nothing

William Shakespeare
Othello

William Shakespeare
Romeo and Juliet

William Shakespeare
The Tempest

Mary Shelley
Frankenstein

Alice Walker
The Color Purple

Tennessee Williams
A Streetcar Named Desire

John Webster
The Duchess of Malfi

GCSE and equivalent levels (£3.50 each)

Harold Brighouse
Hobson's Choice

Charles Dickens
Great Expectations

Charles Dickens
Hard Times

George Eliot
Silas Marner

William Golding
Lord of the Flies

Thomas Hardy
The Mayor of Casterbridge

Susan Hill
I'm the King of the Castle

Barry Hines
A Kestrel for a Knave

Harper Lee
To Kill a Mockingbird

Arthur Miller
A View from the Bridge

Arthur Miller
The Crucible

George Orwell
Animal Farm

J.B. Priestley
An Inspector Calls

J.D. Salinger
The Catcher in the Rye

William Shakespeare
Macbeth

William Shakespeare
The Merchant of Venice

William Shakespeare
Romeo and Juliet

William Shakespeare
Twelfth Night

George Bernard Shaw
Pygmalion

John Steinbeck
Of Mice and Men

Mildred D. Taylor
Roll of Thunder, Hear My Cry

James Watson
Talking in Whispers

A Choice of Poets

Nineteenth Century Short Stories

Poetry of the First World War

Chinua Achebe
Things Fall Apart

Edward Albee
Who's Afraid of Virginia Woolf?

Jane Austen
Mansfield Park

Jane Austen
Northanger Abbey

Jane Austen
Persuasion

Jane Austen
Sense and Sensibility

Samuel Beckett
Waiting for Godot

Alan Bennett
Talking Heads

John Betjeman
Selected Poems

Robert Bolt
A Man for All Seasons

Robert Burns
Selected Poems

Lord Byron
Selected Poems

Geoffrey Chaucer
The Franklin's Tale

Geoffrey Chaucer
The Merchant's Tale

Geoffrey Chaucer
The Miller's Tale

Geoffrey Chaucer
The Nun's Priest's Tale

Geoffrey Chaucer
Prologue to the Canterbury Tales

Samuel Taylor Coleridge
Selected Poems

Daniel Defoe
Moll Flanders

Daniel Defoe
Robinson Crusoe

Shelagh Delaney
A Taste of Honey

Charles Dickens
Bleak House

Charles Dickens
Oliver Twist

Emily Dickinson
Selected Poems

John Donne
Selected Poems

Douglas Dunn
Selected Poems

George Eliot
Middlemarch

George Eliot
The Mill on the Floss

T.S. Eliot
The Waste Land

T.S. Eliot
Selected Poems

Henry Fielding
Joseph Andrews

E.M. Forster
Howards End

E.M. Forster
A Passage to India

John Fowles
The French Lieutenant's Woman

Brian Friel
Translations

Elizabeth Gaskell
North and South

Oliver Goldsmith
She Stoops to Conquer

Graham Greene
Brighton Rock

Thomas Hardy
Jude the Obscure

Thomas Hardy
Selected Poems

Nathaniel Hawthorne
The Scarlet Letter

Ernest Hemingway
The Old Man and the Sea

Homer
The Iliad

Homer
The Odyssey

Aldous Huxley
Brave New World

Ben Jonson
The Alchemist

Ben Jonson
Volpone

James Joyce
A Portrait of the Artist as a Young Man

John Keats
Selected Poems

Philip Larkin
Selected Poems

D.H. Lawrence
The Rainbow

D.H. Lawrence
Sons and Lovers

D.H. Lawrence
Women in Love

Christopher Marlowe
Doctor Faustus

John Milton
Paradise Lost Bks I & II

John Milton
Paradise Lost IV & IX

Sean O'Casey
Juno and the Paycock

George Orwell
Nineteen Eighty-four

John Osborne
Look Back in Anger

Wilfred Owen
Selected Poems

Harold Pinter
The Caretaker

Sylvia Plath
Selected Works

Alexander Pope
Selected Poems

Jean Rhys
Wide Sargasso Sea

William Shakespeare
As You Like It

William Shakespeare
Coriolanus

William Shakespeare
Henry IV Pt 1

William Shakespeare
Henry V

William Shakespeare
Julius Caesar

William Shakespeare
Measure for Measure

William Shakespeare
Much Ado About Nothing

William Shakespeare
A Midsummer Night's Dream

William Shakespeare
Richard II

William Shakespeare
Richard III

William Shakespeare
Sonnets

William Shakespeare
The Taming of the Shrew

William Shakespeare
The Winter's Tale

George Bernard Shaw
Arms and the Man

George Bernard Shaw
Saint Joan

Richard Brinsley Sheridan
The Rivals

Muriel Spark
The Prime of Miss Jean Brodie

John Steinbeck
The Grapes of Wrath

John Steinbeck
The Pearl

Tom Stoppard
Rosencrantz and Guildenstern are Dead

Jonathan Swift
Gulliver's Travels

John Millington Synge
The Playboy of the Western World

W.M. Thackeray
Vanity Fair

Virgil
The Aeneid

Derek Walcott
Selected Poems

Oscar Wilde
The Importance of Being Earnest

Tennessee Williams
Cat on a Hot Tin Roof

Tennessee Williams
The Glass Menagerie

Virginia Woolf
Mrs Dalloway

Virginia Woolf
To the Lighthouse

William Wordsworth
Selected Poems

W.B. Yeats
Selected Poems

York Notes – the Ultimate Literature Guides

York Notes are recognised as the best literature study guides.
If you have enjoyed using this book and have found it useful, you
can now order others directly from us – simply follow the ordering
instructions below.

HOW TO ORDER

Decide which title(s) you require and then order in one of the following
ways:

Booksellers
All titles available from good bookstores.

By post
List the title(s) you require in the space provided overleaf,
select your method of payment, complete your name and
address details and return your completed order form and
payment to:

> *Addison Wesley Longman Ltd*
> *PO BOX 88*
> *Harlow*
> *Essex CM19 5SR*

By phone
Call our Customer Information Centre on 01279 623923 to
place your order, quoting mail number: HEYN1.

By fax
Complete the order form overleaf, ensuring you fill in your
name and address details and method of payment, and fax it
to us on 01279 414130.

By e-mail
E-mail your order to us on awlhe.orders@awl.co.uk listing
title(s) and quantity required and providing full name and
address details as requested overleaf. Please quote mail
number: HEYN1. Please do not send credit card details by
e-mail.

York Notes Order Form

Titles required:

Quantity	Title/ISBN	Price

Sub total _____
Please add £2.50 postage & packing _____
(*P & P is free for orders over £50*) _____
Total _____

Mail no: HEYN1

Your Name _____

Your Address _____

Postcode _____ Telephone _____

Method of payment

☐ I enclose a cheque or a P/O for £_____ made payable to Addison Wesley Longman Ltd

☐ Please charge my Visa/Access/AMEX/Diners Club card
Number _____ Expiry Date _____
Signature _____ Date _____

(please ensure that the address given above is the same as for your credit card)

Prices and other details are correct at time of going to press but may change without notice. All orders are subject to status.

☐ *Please tick this box if you would like a complete listing of Longman Study Guides (suitable for GCSE and A-level students)*

York Press

Longman

Addison Wesley Longman